Grounded Spirituality

Grounded Spirituality

*Aspects of Rabbinic Culture in
its Late Antique Context*

MARC HIRSHMAN

OXFORD
UNIVERSITY PRESS

Oxford University Press is a department of the University of Oxford.
It furthers the University's objective of excellence in research, scholarship,
and education by publishing worldwide. Oxford is a registered trade mark of
Oxford University Press in the UK and in certain other countries.

Published in the United States of America by Oxford University Press
198 Madison Avenue, New York, NY 10016, United States of America.

© Oxford University Press 2025

All rights reserved. No part of this publication may be reproduced, stored in a retrieval system, transmitted, used for text and data mining, or used for training artificial intelligence, in any form or by any means, without the prior permission in writing of Oxford University Press, or as expressly permitted by law, by license or under terms agreed with the appropriate reprographics rights organization. Inquiries concerning reproduction outside the scope of the above should be sent to the Rights Department, Oxford University Press, at the address above.

You must not circulate this work in any other form
and you must impose this same condition on any acquirer

Library of Congress Cataloging-in-Publication Data
Names: Hirshman, Marc, author.
Title: Grounded spirituality : aspects of rabbinic culture in its late
antique context / Marc Hirshman.
Description: First edition. | New York : Oxford University Press, 2025. |
Includes bibliographical references and index. |
Identifiers: LCCN 2024044938 (print) | LCCN 2024044939 (ebook) |
ISBN 9780197660584 (hardback) | ISBN 9780197660614 |
ISBN 9780197660607 (epub)
Subjects: LCSH: Rabbinical literature—History and criticism. |
Jewish literature—Influence.
Classification: LCC BM496.6 .H57 2025 (print) | LCC BM496.6 (ebook) |
DDC 296.109—dc23/eng/20241106
LC record available at https://lccn.loc.gov/2024044938
LC ebook record available at https://lccn.loc.gov/2024044939

DOI: 10.1093/9780197660614.001.0001

Printed by Integrated Books International, United States of America

Contents

Acknowledgments   vii

1. Introduction   1
2. "Torah from Sinai": From the Book of Jubilees to the Babylonian Talmud and Beyond   9
3. Charity: A Capital Matter   21
4. Love and Passion: Between Earth and Heaven   35
5. Philosophy in Rabbinic Circles: More Than Meets the Eye?   47
6. Mysticism and Rabban Yoḥanan ben Zakkai   58
7. The Language of Creation: An Enduring Power   70
8. Torah Study: A Double-Edged Sword   83
9. Why Does Tannaitic Universalism Leave No Trace in Amoraic Literature?   95
10. "This Is My Lord and I Will Glorify": Rabbinic Religiosity   106

      Epilogue: Why Study Late Antique Judaism   114

Notes   121
Index   135
Rabbinic Sources   139

Acknowledgments

These studies began as an honors course in the humanities on Judaism, at the Hebrew University. My friend and colleague David Satran, who headed the Amirim honors program, gave me that wonderful opportunity. I was also privileged to teach the course in English at the University of Chicago as the Joyce Zeger Greenberg visiting professor in Jewish Studies in 2019. It was a comment by one my students there that inspired me to commit the course to writing. It was a pleasure to return annually for a number of years to Stockholm to teach this same course to the Paideia Fellows from all over Europe. I had the privilege of giving a series of online lectures, based on this book, for Beit Avi Hai in Jerusalem this past fall.

My ḥavrutot, David Satran and Deborah Gera, were generous enough to read a draft of the book. I am most grateful, and the book is much improved by their contributions. Every good class usually produces a new insight, and I am thankful to bright and inquisitive students for their insights. The anonymous reader for Oxford University Press read the penultimate draft of this work, and I am very appreciative of the insightful comments offered by that reader. Steve Wiggins and Laura Santo, editors of OUP, and Gopinath Anbalagan and the team of OUP have been, as in my previous books, efficient and solicitous and I am in their debt. Roi Ziv and Levana Chayes were my research assistants and were very helpful in issues of research and editing, and I owe them my thanks. Don Finkel of Leshon Lemudim prepared the index. Part of chapter 7 appeared in a Festschrift in honor of Professor David Stern.

As always, family and friends inspire me to try to bring the riches of Jewish, Christian, and Greco-Roman literatures to inform and enhance the thinking of my twenty-first-century readers. My sister

Debby and brother Harold and his wife Lorie Chaiten and sister-in law Chaya in the USA and their families have overcome the proverb of a distant sibling (Proverbs 27,10). I have enjoyed warm collegiality with many, many scholars here in Israel, in Europe, and in the United States. I am grateful to them for all I have learned from them in the study of Judaism, Christianity, and Roman religion in late antiquity.

This book is dedicated with love to Edna, for reasons more than apparent to all who know her. Edna and I cherish the new additions to our family since 2016, our daughter-in-law Naama Erlich, and our grandchildren, Meir, Inbar, Hallel, Naveh, Eli, and Shani. May they all prosper and continue to be a source of joy and goodness.

These are dangerous, unsettling, and heartbreaking times worldwide and most assuredly here at home in Jerusalem. As in my previous works, I end this introduction also with a prayer for peace, that most treasured and elemental of blessings: "To life: Peace to you, peace to your household, and to all that is yours peace" (1 Sam 25:6).

1
Introduction

The formative period of rabbinic religion, 1–500 CE, is roughly parallel to what classical historians of the past fifty years call late antiquity. The history of religion in late antiquity has flourished and has enriched our understanding of rabbinic religion. The Jewish sages of the first five centuries of the first millennium of the Common Era forged a religion that combined the ethereal and the mundane in what I think is exceptional in the history of religions.[1] This balance, combined with a passion for learning and education, enabled a conquered people in exile and those who remained disenfranchised in their own land to persevere and flourish over the next two millennia. In a previous work, *The Stabilization of Rabbinic Culture* (OUP, 2009), I depicted and analyzed major sections of the Midrash and Talmud that concentrated on education. In this book, I describe interesting and sometimes unique aspects of rabbinic religiosity, through a series of short studies on a variety of subjects in rabbinic thought and practice. In each chapter, I focus on one rabbinic text while making reference to some others in rabbinic literature that share the same theme. I have also tried to give a sense of how the rabbinic attitudes compare to Greco-Roman literature or to Christian thought of late antiquity or both, and I hope that references to scholarly works in those fields will allow the reader to continue that avenue of research.

I will briefly survey the oral literature of the rabbis of late antiquity and clarify some of the main terms. The rabbinic period is divided into the earlier Tannaitic period (1–250 CE) and the later Amoraic period (225–500 CE), and I will describe the works produced in those two respective periods. I will then outline two methodological issues of import when dealing with these texts and with rabbinic religiosity in general. Finally, I will survey the contents of this book.

Rabbinic learning of the first five centuries of the Common Era was for the most part an oral affair, edited in oral anthologies.[2] The scholars of the first half of the period, called *tannaim* (reciters, learners), presumably edited their own individual collections of the legal tradition classified according to subject, in a form we call Mishna. Eventually Judah the Patriarch's edition of the Mishna, divided into six orders and subdivided into sixty topical tractates, became the authoritative Mishna at the beginning of the third century. There is a tannaitic companion volume to the Mishna called the Tosefta (=supplement). It was edited a generation later and acts as a commentary and expansion to the parallel sections of the Mishna, having a similar structure to the Mishna. It contains also additional material of tannaitic origin not found in the Mishna. Recent scholarship has shown that often this later collection actually contains earlier formulations of some of the Mishna laws before they were edited and redacted by Judah the Patriarch.[3]

During this same Tannaitic period of some two hundred years, another form of rabbinic learning flourished called Midrash, that studied the oral law as it related to the last four of the five books of the Torah (Genesis being predominantly nonlegal narrative). Thus, there evolved two schools of Midrash Tannaim (sometimes referred to as *Midrash Halacha* = Midrash of the Law), identified with the second-century luminaries, R. Akiva and R. Yishmael.[4] We have distinct midrashic collections, edited by the two "schools" associated with R. Akiva and R. Yishmael, respectively, for each of those four books of the Torah. Some scholars hold that some of these collections were written. Though these collections focus on legal issues, there is a substantial amount of aggadic midrash—that is, scriptural interpretation which attends to nonlegal matters, such as ethics, religious thought, and even anecdotes. Literally, *aggada* or *hagaddah* translates as "speech or rhetoric." The aggadic material is more extensive in the tannaitic collections on Exodus and Deuteronomy but almost nonexistent in the collections on Leviticus. Aggadic midrash dilates on Scripture to produce stories, apothegms, and lessons of an ethical, moral, pedagogic, and sometimes simply rhetorical nature.

By the third century CE, Jewish sages in the Land of Israel and also in Babylonia, recited, studied, discussed, and commented on the Mishna of Rabbi Judah the Patriarch, again preferring oral learning. These sages, the *amoraim* (speakers), flourished in those two geographic locations, with some sages traveling back and forth between the two centers. Their comments and discussions, along with unattributed, "anonymous" (*stam*) discussions, comprise the Talmud or Gemara, an oral work that was later written down in the Geonic period (seventh–eleventh century CE). These discussions included analyses of *baraitot*—additional tannaitic literature not to be found in the Mishna of Rabbi Judah the Patriarch. The *baraitot* cited in the amoraic and later anonymous discussions in the Gemara often are to be found in the Tosefta and the Midrash Tannaim. These *amoraic* discussions, along with many additional legal debates and excursions into nonlegal narratives and Scripture, were eventually edited orally into the Talmuds. The Jerusalem Talmud was compiled orally in the last decade of the fourth century, mainly in the Galilee but also in scholarly centers in Caesarea, Lydda, and the Golan. The Babylonian Talmud was compiled orally in various scholarly centers in Babylonia around the sixth century. Modern scholarship has spotlighted the anonymous discourse ("*stam*," "*stama deGemara*") in the Babylonian Talmud, with most scholars seeing it as the last stage of development of our Talmud around the sixth or seventh century.[5] About one-third of the Babylonian Talmud deals with nonlegal matter, which was called *aggada*. Aggada, as mentioned, includes ethical reflections, stories, parables, and rabbinic comments on Scripture. The Jerusalem Talmud has far less aggada since the amoraic sages in the Land of Israel developed special collections devoted to aggada

(Midrash Aggada)—for example, Genesis Rabbah. These Land of Israel special collections of aggada are generally attached to the five books of Moses and the Five Scrolls. One must distinguish between these two terms, *midrash* and *aggada*, which are sometimes, mistakenly, used interchangeably. The word *midrash* describes the procedure of investigating Scripture whether of a legal nature, *halacha*, or nonlegal, *aggada*. Aggada is a catchall term to describe the content of all rabbinic teaching that was nonlegal in nature.

I wish to raise two methodological issues that need clarification in any work dealing with the vast rabbinic literature of late antiquity, mostly oral as noted, though there is early evidence in the Talmud for *written aggadic books*. The first issue is the veracity of attributions of sayings to a particular sage and that sage's biography. This is a thorny problem, which has been raised time and again and debated in critical scholarship for the last fifty years. Another major methodological issue is the relation of this rabbinic literature to the burgeoning Christian movement, which developed in this period from being a persecuted offshoot of Judaism, vehemently opposed by the Roman rulers and many Jewish sages, to the recognized religion of that same Roman Empire.

Over fifty years ago, the notion that one could rely on the accuracy of a certain statement, legal or aggadic, actually belonging to or originating with the particular sage who said it, was challenged by scholars in a variety of disciplines.[6] Historians who had hoped to explain statements within their historical circumstances were challenged both by the fact that often attributions varied in different manuscripts or in parallel quotes. There is a famous passage in the Jerusalem Talmud that advises on citing sources. If one can cite the sages back to Moses, then cite them; otherwise cite either the first or last sage (j. Kiddushin 1:7 61a). Thus, it is clear from this firsthand evidence that ascription of a statement to a sage does not mean that it necessarily was created during that sage's lifetime or necessarily reacts to the historical circumstances of that sage. The problem of tying a certain view to its historical setting becomes more challenging and less certain. Richard Kalmin has achieved a sensitive and perceptive view of the issue.[7] Yet even if the attribution was authentic, a different problem continued to raise some doubts. The degree of literary crafting and fashioning of rabbinic literature was the subject of numerous studies over the past hundred years, thus calling into question whether the language of the statement attributed to a certain sage was indeed that sage's statement or a restatement by the editor of the Midrash or Talmudic section. This two-pronged challenge, together with many anonymous statements in rabbinic literature, sets a high bar when trying to tie specific statements to their historical setting.

What I have chosen to do in each chapter is to isolate a particularly rich and poignant passage that treats an important topic in rabbinic religion. I analyze it in depth and reflect on it sometimes in light of other treatments in rabbinic literature and usually try to enrich it with a comparison to Greco-Roman or Christian literature of the period. We will meet in these chapters two of the greatest tannaim: Rabban Yoḥanan ben Zakkai, who is credited with the spiritual restoration in the aftermath of the destruction of the temple (70 CE); and R. Akiva, the preeminent scholar who supported the disastrous Bar Kochva revolt some sixty years later. It is the vibrant spiritual and religious lessons that emerge from these sources that we try to evoke, through critical study, in the following pages.

The second methodological issue is the degree of cross-fertilization between the Jewish sages of the first half of the first millennium of the Common Era and their Christian (and Jewish-Christian) counterparts. The current conventional wisdom is that the so-called parting of the ways between Judaism and Christianity occurred much later than previously thought.[8] I remain convinced that Christians and Jewish Christians were marked as "the other" quite early in our period, sometime in the second century CE, even if this did not necessarily entail formal ostracizing or cutting all ties. One of the earliest and most famous stories concerning interaction is of the great R. Eliezer ben Hyrcanus, Rabban Yoḥanan's student and R. Akiva's teacher, who conversed with a Christian about a religious topic (t. Ḥullin 2:24). Clearly, given the setting and moral of the story, it was told to dissuade others from entering into conversation with Christians. Yet retelling of the account is evidence at the very least of an effort to squelch dialogue that was apparently ongoing. So, too, other stories and even some laws (e.g., t. Ḥullin 2:20–21) were told and enacted to distance Jews from Christians and their reputed powers of healing. On the Christian side, we find prominent Christian scholars, Origen in Caesarea in the mid-third century and St. Jerome in Bethlehem at the end of the fourth century, in dialogue with Jews. Whether Justin Martyr's "Dialogue with Trypho the Jew," written in Rome around 150 CE, reflects a real dialogue is doubtful, but it might indicate that such a dialogue was seen as possible. However, it appears that into the last stages of late antiquity there was ongoing dialogue between the two religions.[9]

Now, I will survey the contents of this volume on rabbinic religiosity. The first chapter explores the strikingly different views on what transpired in the forty days and nights Moses spent on Mount Sinai. The texts in this chapter range from Second Temple times through the closing of late antiquity. Each text gives pride of place to that source's conception of what was central to its own religious thought. In the following chapter on charity, a subject thoroughly researched over the past two decades, I survey and analyze a unique view in the Jerusalem Talmud's treatment of the subject.[10] It is true that the position staked out there might simply be a rhetorical move, but rhetoric was employed in antiquity to persuade and convince, while entertaining. Here, too, the pragmatism of the rabbinic view coupled with the primacy of charity is quite impressive.

Chapter 4 contrasts Rabbi Akiva's famous dicta on love—loving God and one's neighbor above all and his view that the Song of Songs as being the Holiest of Scripture—with a startling and disconcerting aggadic midrash. A famous sage of the Amoraic period in the Land of Israel (225 CE–400 CE), Rabbi Simon ben Lakish, emphasizes a very earthy religious passion. His statement has an interesting parallel in his Christian contemporary, the mid-third-century Caesarean church father, Origen. We know that Origen was in touch with learned Jewish sages, and we also know that some of the Jewish sages were highly conversant in Greek, with R. Abbahu of Caesarea, Origen's younger contemporary, being one of the parade examples. Yet there is remarkably little mention of formal Greek philosophy in rabbinic literature, despite the use of almost three thousand Greek and Latin loanwords. Chapter 5 analyzes a singular dialogue in the Mishna Avot, in light of Judah Goldin's provocative essay claiming that there was a philosophic session in Rabban Yoḥanan ben Zakkai's academy. We go on to consider the place of philosophy in rabbinic literature.

The next two chapters, Chapters 6 and 7, move on to the place of mysticism in the rabbinic worldview. There has been an enormous and prodigious outpouring of research on the subject in the past seventy-five years. Chapter 6 treats the classic story of that same great first-century sage, Rabban Yoḥanan ben Zakkai, and the place of esotericism within his scholarly pursuits. In Chapter 7, I engage the subject of God's creation through speech, Hebrew speech according to many, and how much of that creative power of the Hebrew language remained concealed and available in the Hebrew Torah.

Chapter 8 explores a new theme that emerges in late tannaitic times—the possible danger involved in Torah study. I suggest that this might have been a response or polemic with the burgeoning Christian movement. In Chapter 9, we describe what appears to be the disappearance of any trace of universalism in amoraic thought, though it had been present, to some extent, in tannaitic literature. A clear picture of a tannaitic school of thought (Tannaitic period, 1–250 CE, Land of Israel) that espoused a universalistic ideology emerged from a number of scholarly studies over the past forty years. I ponder why that universalism all but disappears in the second half of the rabbinic period, called the Amoraic period (Babylonian Amoraim, 225–500 CE: Israel Amoraim, 225–400 CE).

Chapter 10 focuses on a tannaitic midrash commenting on the Song at the Sea (Exodus 15) that beautifully encapsulates different forms of rabbinic religiosity. It would seem that the revelation at Sinai generated manifold variations on its themes throughout history. In the brief epilogue, I reflect on the import of rabbinic literature in our own time.

2

"Torah from Sinai"

From the Book of Jubilees to the Babylonian Talmud and Beyond

What happened during those forty days and nights Moses spent on Mount Sinai? The lean account of the Torah (Exod 34:28; Deut 9:9–12) gave ample room to fill in the gap and tweaked the imagination of Jewish thinkers before and after the destruction of the Second Temple in 70 CE. Their accounts are strikingly different. We will begin with the most famous legend attributed to the third-century CE preeminent Babylonian sage, Rav. We will go on to compare it to the extraordinary Second Temple book of Jubilees and briefly peruse the Palestinian midrashic account of the sixth and seventh centuries CE, recorded in the Tanchuma collection. The Hebrew story in the Babylonian Talmud b. Menaḥot 29b may be translated as follows:[1]

> R. Judah said that Rav said: At the time when Moses ascended on high he found the Holy One Blessed be He sitting and tying crowns to the letters.
>
> He said before Him, "Master of the Universe! Who detains (*meakev*) you?"
>
> He said to him, "There is a person, who will be (*atid lihiyot*) at the end of many generations and Akiva ben Joseph is his name, who will expound (*atid lidrosh*) on each and every tip and tip mounds upon mounds of laws."
>
> He said before Him, "Master of the Universe! Show him to me."

He said to him, "Turn back." He went and sat at the end of eighteen rows of students but he did not understand what they were saying. His strength failed him. When they reached an issue, they said, "Our master (R. Akiva), from where to you (what is your source)?" He said to them, "It is a law of Moses from Sinai." His (Moses's) mind was set at ease. He returned before the Holy One Blessed be He.

He said to him, "Master of the Universe! You have a person like this and you give the Torah by me?" He said to him, "Silence, thus arose in thought before me."

He said before Him, "Master of the Universe! You showed me his Torah, show me his reward." He said to him, "Turn back." He saw they were weighing his flesh in the butcher shop.

He said before him, "Master of the Universe! This is Torah and this is its reward?" He said to him, "Silence. Thus arose in thought before me."

First, the *mise-en-scène*:

The Hebrew opening, "When Moses *ascended on high (alah lamarom)*," echoes a very similar formulation in Ps 68, which also describes the mountain of God and Sinai. The verse, "*You went up to the heights (alita lamarom)*, having taken captives, having received tribute of humans" (Ps 68:19) was applied by rabbinic sages to Moses's ascent to Sinai.[2] The motif of "when Moses ascended on high" recurs three more times at b. Shabbat 88b–89a, in a medley of musings by R. Joshua ben Levi, Rav's Israel colleague, one of which rehearses the same scene of Moses upon arrival "finding God attaching crowns to the letters."

We'll pause here to make two cardinal points concerning late antique rabbinic literature. Elementary education in rabbinic times consisted of mastering Scripture. Many, if not all of the Jewish sages, often spoke with and through biblical verses, as a vehicle to convey their thoughts. Second, a full appreciation of a particular sage's interpretations or literary creations demands scouring the rabbinic corpus for similar and dissimilar treatments. These two contexts—biblical allusions and parallel treatments—help give a fuller sense of the range of meanings in the sage's homily or story. As we will see, there is a sea change in the use of that same opening scene as developed by R. Joshua ben Levi in b. Shabbat, as opposed to R. Judah in the name of Rav here in b. Menaḥot.

Jonah Fraenkel, the Hebrew University scholar who pioneered the literary analysis of rabbinic stories in the latter third of the twentieth century, analyzed this story. He pointed out that God stages the scene to arouse Moses's curiosity as to why, when he finally makes it up the mountain, the Torah is not quite ready ("Should I come back?" Moses must have mused, as I read it).[3] I might also suggest that the extra adornment of the letters is a tacit answer to the question of what took forty days and nights, causing Moses to tarry so long. These adornments became part and parcel of the scribal art for writing Torah scrolls and were summed up, a few lines after our story, by the mid-forth-century sage Rava (or Raba): "seven letters (of the Torah) require three 'zayinim'" (lit. the Hebrew letter *zayin*; fig. crowns or decorations).

The story revolves around Moses's five queries or requests, all with the same formulation—"He said before Him, 'Master of the Universe!'" God's response is immediate, but in the final two peremptory and strident—"Silence (or "Be quiet" or more coarsely "Shut up"), that is what entered (lit. ascended) my mind (lit. in thought before me)." Moses does not understand God's decisions. In my paraphrase, Moses queries, if there is to be someone as great as Akiva, why then does God view Moses as deserving to be the receiver of the Torah? This dovetails nicely with Moses's legendary humility (Num 12:3). His follow-up question is "How can such a great man suffer such a terrible end?" God's ways of reward and punishment are as incomprehensible to Moses as is Akiva's own oral Torah, despite the fact that in Akiva's view the particular law (*halacha*) that was being discussed and which Moses failed to grasp was a law given to Moses *from Sinai*. God acquiesces to Moses's first three requests, two of which are visual requests, "show me," but the final two are rebuffed with the curt, "be quiet, thus arose in thought before me." Moses ascended to Sinai but cannot ascend to God's thought.

Here, too, the sages are echoing the language of the Scripture's description of Moses's encounter with God at Exodus 33:18. Moses asks God: "*Show me* your Presence (*kevodecha*)," and the response later in that chapter is a list of God's "thirteen" attributes of justice and mercy, the elusive key as it were to God's approach to reward and punishment.

The Talmudic story has intertwined two major themes. One is the gaping chasm between divine justice and human ability to fathom it, and the other, the continuity, yet discontinuity, of the written Torah received by Moses and the oral Torah of R. Akiva, some 1,500 years later.

We will now turn to R. Joshua ben Levi's very different rendering of that very same scene of Moses viewing God attaching crowns to the letters of Torah. At b. Shabbat 89a, we read:

> And R. Joshua ben Levi said, At the time when Moses ascended on high he found the Holy One Blessed be He tying crowns to the letters
>
> Said the Holy One Blessed be He to Moses, "Moses, is there no greeting (*ein shalom*) in your town?"
>
> He said before Him, "Is there a servant who greets (*notein shalom*) his master?"
>
> He (i.e., God) said to him, "You should have helped me!"
>
> Immediately[4] he said, "and now let the power of the Lord be great" (Num 14:17).

In this vignette, Moses the faithful servant waits quietly, watching God's activity, and it is God who begins the conversation with a question, literally translated, "Moses, is there no peace (*shalom*) in your town?" This is the equivalent of, "Moses, don't they say hello where you come from?" Moses replies, "Is there a servant who greets (lit. "gives peace to") his master?" To which God responds, "You should have helped me." Immediately Moses says "and now let the power of the Lord be great." Moses according to this version is enjoined to empower God, and he does so by quoting to God the verse from the book of Numbers that introduces God's thirteen attributes of justice and mercy. That verse would become a centerpiece of Jewish liturgy, especially on the high holidays. In this account, then, there is a partnering of the divine and the human rather than the infinite distancing in our first story. Strikingly different theologies are at play in these two narratives, both invoking directly and indirectly, the scene in Exodus where Moses asks to understand God's ways and is told God's ways of justice and mercy in God's passing presence.

Joshua ben Levi's preceding homily in that same Talmudic periscope, sugya, in Shabbat portrays God as instructing Moses "when he ascends on high" to reply to the angels' challenge as to what is the place of a mortal among them and the reason that God's treasured Torah be given to a mortal. Both of R Joshua's homilies are set "on high" and have Moses being challenged, once by the angels and then by God. Interestingly the common thread between the angels' challenge and the R. Akiva/Moshe narrative is the question of who can possibly merit receiving God's word.

Let us now turn to the Second Temple rendering of Moses's stay on Sinai. The book of Jubilees is an early second-century BCE rewrite of the Torah, focusing on Genesis and the first part of Exodus. In a real tour de force the book begins, not at Gen 1:1 as expected but with Moses on Sinai:

> In the first year of the Exodus of the children of Israel from Egypt, in the third month on the sixteenth day, The Lord spoke to Moses, saying "Come to me on the mountain and I shall give you the two stone tablets of the Law and commandment, which I have written, so that you may teach them." (Jub 1:1).

The prologue uses material from the accounts in Exodus and Deuteronomy but sets out clearly the author and the setting of the giving of the Torah. This contrasts with the Bible itself that begins in media res without identifying either the speaker or the setting. Jubilees's prologue goes on to record that Moses was on the mountain forty days and nights but gives a very different depiction of what took place for those long days and nights—"And the Lord revealed to him both what was in the beginning and what will occur" (Jub 1:4). The prologue continues with references to Deuteronomy's description of Israel's eventual veering from the path and eventually to repentance and the ultimate restoration of the everlasting Temple. Moses is instructed to write the contents of everything revealed to him on the mountain. Moreover, according to Jubilees, God commands the angel of presence to "write for Moses from the first day of creation until my sanctuary is built in their midst for ever and ever" (Jub 1:27). The angel goes on to command Moses, "Write the whole account of creation . . ." (Jub 2:1), and we are then treated to a much more embellished and detailed account of the story of creation than that preserved in the book of Genesis.

In this account, the forty-day sojourn on Sinai has Moses transcribing the history of the world, presumably as it is set out in the book of Jubilees itself. There is no hint of an oral tradition. All that was and will be, according to this version, was made known to Moses and is written down by him in the forty days atop Sinai.

This Second Temple tradition privileges the written over the oral, whereas the Talmudic tradition, a half millennia later, privileged the oral over the written. But how extensive was the oral revelation on Sinai according to the Talmudic sages? As always, opinions differ.

Let's return to our opening story. R. Akiva tells his students that the source for the law he had stated was "It is a law to Moses from Sinai" (*halacha lemoshe misinai*). This phrase has a calming effect on Moses, who had listened to the class cluelessly. What does the statement "It is a law to Moses from Sinai" mean? If indeed the law's source was Moses, why doesn't Moses understand it? It is clear, as one leading modern scholar has pointed out, that Rav has accorded to the law the same incommensurability as the theological conundrum of the righteous suffering (Akiva) and reward going to the less deserving.[5] Here, too, Moses is the source of the law, but its development and *nachleben* elude him. Moses is unable to comprehend the law as it evolved. Yet his heirs see him as the source of the law, even though they are fully aware that the developed law would no longer be recognizable by the founder.

This is not the only position in Talmudic literature. Other sources, among them a signal one attributed to the same R. Joshua ben Levi quoted above, deem that the oral law in its entirety and final detailed form was revealed to Moses on Sinai. There are then maximalist and minimalist positions in late antiquity as to the extent and provenance of the oral law.[6] Heschel traced this debate to the second-century CE R. Akiva, who was a maximalist, as opposed to his contemporary R. Yishmael, the minimalist. The great twentieth-century Talmudist, E. S. Rosenthal, contextualized this debate within a parallel and contemporary development in Roman law, pitting the school that was bent on preserving the law as opposed to the school that was keen to innovate.[7]

The oral law or oral tradition was a major tenet of Pharisaic Judaism before the destruction of the Second Temple in 70 CE and became the object of intense study, reflection, and development in rabbinic Judaism from the first to the sixth centuries CE. The regnant mode of study in rabbinic circles was oral recitation and oral discussion. Eventually these oral traditions were compiled into the six orders of Mishna and the parallel Tosefta compilation. At the same time, a second possibly competing form of study existed in rabbinic circles. This was predicated on deriving and attaching both oral law and aggadic lore to scripture. This other form was compiled into the tannaitic midrash of the mid-third century CE and possibly even circulated in written form, though this is far from certain.[8]

The oral traditions were a flashpoint of controversy well into the Middle Ages (if not to our own day), and their validity and authority were hotly debated throughout. Josephus asserts that the Saducees did not accept the oral traditions.[9] Some scholars assert that Jesus, as portrayed in Mark 7, for example, denied the validity of the oral extension of purity laws while respecting the Mosaic purity laws![10] Might we consider the debate over the oral law among rival Jewish factions and the growing Christian presence in Palestine as a possible explanation for the differing views of Rav and R. Joshua ben Levi in the accounts above? The former resided in third-century Babylonia after having spent years of study with the editor of the Mishna, Judah the Patriarch, in Palestine. Might the surging of the Jewish and pagan followers of Jesus have resulted in reifying the antiquity of the entire oral law by R. Joshua ben Levi?

R. Joshua ben Levi stakes out, in another source, the maximalist position. He holds that "Mikra, Mishna, Talmud, and Aggada, even what an experienced disciple will instruct before his master was already said to Moses at Sinai" (y. Pe'ah 2:6, 17a). Was this extreme position designed to counter the Christian claim that the traditional Jewish interpretation of the Hebrew Bible had been superseded by the Christian exegesis that saw the Torah as a coded prophecy of the coming of their messiah, Jesus?[11] This radical position has its roots in R. Akiva's theology a half century earlier that advocated a maximalist position. There is a touch of irony that it is the maximalist Akiva who is the protagonist of Rav's account of Moses on Sinai that portrays Moses as unable to understand Akiva's Torah. But the question remains. Was this maximalist approach an answer to the opponents of the oral law from Second Temple times through Christianity of late antiquity?

The answer to that tantalizing question, in relation to the third-century R. Joshua ben Levi, must remain in doubt, but the latest iteration of the motif of Moses on Sinai in the Palestinian Tanchuma midrash (sixth or seventh century CE) gives an unequivocal answer. There we read:

> R. Judah bar Shalom said: When the Holy One told Moses *"write down"* (Ex. 34:27), the latter wanted the Mishna also to be in writing. However the Holy One blessed is He foresaw that time would come when the nations of the world would translate the Torah and read it in Greek and then say: "We are Israel," and now the scales are balanced. The Holy One blessed is He will then say to the nations: you contend that you are my children. That may be, but only those who possess my mysteries are my children, i.e. [those who have] the *Mishna* which is given orally.[12]

Professor Lieberman goes on to unpack this source:

> By the fourth century the Christian Bible had already long since been published: it was accessible and open to anyone who could read. The Jewish oral law remained recorded in secret (private) rolls and in private codices. It constituted the mysteries of the Lord which were published *orally* only for Israel.[13]

Lieberman had proven in the chapter to which these quotes were appended in an appendix that the official publication of the Mishna was an oral affair, and there was no written authoritative version of Mishna.

Summary

The Mishna states, "Moses received the Torah from Sinai" (m. Avot 1:1). It was, in that view, passed down orally generation to generation through the end of the Tannaitic period (c. 250 CE) and beyond. How comprehensive was that oral Torah? How authoritative was that oral Torah? The Jewish sages of the first five centuries whose views were compiled in the Mishna, Tosefta, Midrash, and Talmud were unanimous in advocating the supremacy of the oral Torah. It was Israel's unique and inimitable link to God, the keeper of God's secrets, at least according to the Tanchuma midrash. This was at one and the same time the ultimate marker of rabbinic identity and the object of constant study and devotion. God labored to prepare the Torah for the great rabbinic sage Akiva, while Moses looked on (impatiently?) and was not destined to comprehend Akiva's Torah. This oral tradition exalted in diversity and debate. The oral law and lore were the bone of contention between the rabbinic movement and its detractors.

Within the rabbinic movement, there was no agreement as to the extent of the original oral revelation. Were all the future developments and permutations of the oral Torah already given to Moses at Sinai? Or did the oral Torah of Sinai consist of general rules and principles that were to be applied to the written Torah in future generations?[14]

Usually this issue is discussed within the context of the development of rabbinic halacha, the law, but it is no less relevant to the development of aggada, stories and theologies such as those we have seen here relating to Moses at Sinai. How much of this vast and sometimes contradictory storehouse of legend and stories interpreting and refracting Scripture were stories handed down for generations? When did Jews begin telling stories about Moses on Sinai?

By way of contrast, one can note the late first-century general turned historian Josephus, conjecturing for his Roman audience what took place in those forty days on Sinai:

> And he proceeded to disclose the care which God had for them, telling them that He had during these days shown him that manner of government which would promote their happiness and that he desired that a tabernacle should be made for Him,

whither He would descend whensoever He came among them, "to the intent," said He, "that when we move elsewhere we may take this with us and have no more need to ascend to Sinai. . . ." Having so said, he showed them two tablets on which were graven the ten words, five on either of them, and the writing thereon was from the hand of God (*Jewish Antiquities* 3: 99–101, Loeb ed., pp. 363–365).

Josephus's account hews close to the story line of Scripture—with the appointing of judges and officials preceding the Ten Commandments and the instructions for building the tabernacle following nearby. In so doing, he diverges from Jubilees and the story in Menahot that depicted Sinai as an event of forecasting the future, not only giving the law.

References

Boyarin, Daniel (2019), "Mark 7. 1–23 Finally," in Taylor G. Petrey et al. (eds.), *Re-Making the World: Christianity and Categories—Essays in Honor of Karen L. King* (Tübingen: Mohr Siebeck): 19–34.

Fraenkel, Jonah (1977–78), "Hermeneutic Questions in the Study of the Aggadic Narrative," (Hebrew) *Tarbiz* 47: 157–172.

Halivni, David (1991), *Peshat and Derash: Plain and Applied Meaning in Rabbinic Exegesis* (New York: Oxford).

Heschel, Abraham Joshua (2005), *Heavenly Torah as Refracted Through the Generations*, edited and translated from the Hebrew with commentary by Gordon Tucker with Leonard Levin (New York and London: Continuum).

Kister, Menahem (2021), "Jots and Tittles," *Eretz-Israel: Archaeological, Historical and Geographical Studies* 34: 147–55.

Lieberman, Saul (1962), *Hellenism in Jewish Palestine*, second improved edition (New York: The Jewish Theological Seminary of America).

Rosenthal, Eliezer Shimshon (2021), "Tradition and Innovation in the Halacha of the Sages," (Hebrew) in Eliezer Shimshon Rosenthal, *Studies in Talmudic Literature* (Hebrew) (Jerusalem: Magnes Press): 739–792 (= *Tarbiz* 63 1994: 321–374).

Rubenstein, Jeffery (2010), *Stories of the Babylonian Talmud* (Baltimore: The Johns Hopkins University Press).

Urbach, Ephraim Elimelech (1947), "Halacha and Prophecy," (Hebrew) *Tarbiz* 18: 1–27.

Zussman, Yaakov (2005), "Torah She-Be-'al-Pe'—Peshuta Ke-Mashma'a," in Yaakov Zussman and David Rosenthal (eds.), *Mehqere Talmud* (Vol. 3; Jerusalem: Magnes Press): 209–384.

3
Charity
A Capital Matter

In an oft-quoted letter,[1] the emperor Julian, attempting to overturn the Christian conversion of the Roman Empire under Constantine some fifty years earlier, exhorted a pagan priest:

> I order that one-fifth of this be used for the poor who serve the priests, and the remainder be distributed by us to strangers and beggars. For it is disgraceful that, when no Jew ever has to beg, and the impious Galileans support not only their own poor but ours as well, all men see that our people lack aid from us.[2]

Even if we allow for rhetorical hyperbole, Julian's praise of Jews and Christians ("the impious Galileans") for their care of the needy is impressive.[3]

Commandments to be charitable and engage in acts of lovingkindness are prominent in numerous passages of the Torah, Prophets, and Writings. Those commandments were amplified by stories and apothegms in the Prophets and Writings. The message of the book of Ruth was summed up by the rabbinic sages as teaching "not what is prohibited or permissible" but to teach "the reward due to those who do deeds of lovingkindness."[4] Modern interpreters and the midrash alike read the poetic phrasing of Proverbs 19:17—"He who is generous to the poor, makes a loan to the Lord, He will repay him his due"—not that God's mercy would be given to those who give loans to the poor, but rather one who has mercy on the poor has given a loan to God![5] This emphatic trend was continued in Second Temple literature. The Second Temple book of Tobit tells the tale of a pious Jew, Tobit, who devoted himself to bringing the dead to a proper burial. Beyond which Tobit himself advocates almsgiving.[6] The brilliant Ben Sira says, "a raging fire is extinguished by water, so righteousness (*zedaka*) atones sin."[7]

There has been a prodigious flow of excellent research on charity over the past two decades, including Peter Brown, *Poverty and Leadership in the Later Roman Empire* (2002); Seth Schwartz, *Were the Jews a Mediterranean Society?: Reciprocity and Solidarity in Ancient Judaism* (2010); Gary Anderson's *Charity* (2013); Yael Ben Shalom Wilfand's, *Poverty, Charity and the Image of the Poor in Rabbinic Texts from the Land of Israel* (2014); Alyssa M. Gray, *Charity in Rabbinic Judaism* (2019); Greg Gardner, *Wealth, Poverty, and Charity in Jewish Antiquity* (2022); and others. These major works, each providing a new and insightful conceptualization of charity, have been complemented by a host of important articles on this subject, a subject that has engaged modern scholarship for well over a century (e.g., Urbach 1951).

We will focus on one major collection on charity in the Jerusalem Talmud in the final chapter of Peah. The entire tractate is devoted to detailing the Scriptural commandment of leaving the corner (= *pe'ah*) of one's field for the poor. I hope to show that this selection from the last chapter of the tractate, which deals more generally with charity, has put the idea of charity on a new and entirely different basis.

Mishnah: y. Peah 8:7:
We/They[8] do not give to the poor person who is passing through, from one place to another, less than a loaf that costs a *pundion*, when four *seah* cost a *sela* (equivalent to two meals; Albeck 1957: 65). If he stays overnight, we give him necessities for lodging (bed and pillow; Albeck 1957: 65, Tosefta: oil and legumes). If he stays over the Sabbath, we give him food for three meals.

He, who has food for two meals, should not take from the *tamḥui* (communal platter, i.e., soup kitchen). If, for fourteen meals, he should not take from the *kupa* (money basket). The *kupa* is collected by two people and distributed by three.

Halakah (=Gemara):
Tamḥui, every day; the *kupa*, from *erev shabbat* to *erev shabbat*. *Tamḥui* is for everybody, the *kupa* is only for local people exclusively. R. Ḥuna said, "the *tamḥui* (is collected) by three people, because it is (given out) on the spot."

R. Ḥelbo in the name of R. Ba bar Zavda, "We do not set up less than three *parnasim* (communal functionaries[9]). Come[10] and see, monetary cases (are adjudicated) by three, capital cases (lit. cases of *lives*) how much more so!" (If so) Let them be twenty-three (as in capital judgments)? Until one assembles them, he (the poor person) is in danger.

Rabbi Yose in the name of Rabbi Yoḥanan: "We do not set up two brothers as *parnasim*." Rabbi Yose removed one of two brothers. He entered and said before them: "There was not found in that person any transgression, but we do not set up two brothers as *parnasim*." Rabbi Yose went up to Kufra and wanted to set up *parnasim* there, but they did not take it upon themselves. He came and said before them: 'Ben Bavai over the oakum' (m. Sheqalim 5:1). Just like this one (i.e., Ben Bavai), who was appointed over the wicks, merited to be counted among the greats of his generation, you who are being *appointed over the lives of people*, how much more so." R. Ḥaggai, when he set up *parnasim*, would have them lift up the Torah,[11] as to say that every public office that is given, is given by the Torah (Prov 8:15-16): "Through me, kings rule, through me, princes become princes." R. Ḥiyya bar Ba set up *archonin*, "members of the governing body of the city council."[12]

R. Lezer was *parnas*. Once, he went home. He said to them: What have you been doing? They said to him, "a group

came, and they ate and drank and prayed for you." He said to them, "That is not a good reward." Another time, he came home and said to them: "What have you been doing?" They said to him, "another group came, and they ate and drank and cursed you. He said to them, "Now that is a good reward."
They wanted to appoint R. Akiva *parnas*. He said, "we will take counsel at home." They followed him and heard his voice saying: "on condition to be cursed, on condition to be insulted."
R. Ba bar Zavda said: Rav and R. Yoḥanan disagreed. One said, "we scrutinize (the recipient, when giving) clothing but do not scrutinize (when giving) *for the lives of the souls*." The other said, "even (when giving clothing) we do not scrutinize, because of the covenant of Abraham our father...."

Mishnah: y. Peah 8:8:
Someone who has two hundred *zuz* should not take gleanings, forgotten sheaves, *pe'ah*, and tithes of the poor. If one had two hundred minus one dinar (= one zuz), even if a thousand people gave him at the same time, he should take.

Mishnah: y. Peah 8:9:
Someone who has fifty zuz, and buys and sells with them—this one should not take.
Everyone who should not take but takes, will not leave this world until he will be in need of people's help. But everyone who should take but does not take, will not die of old age until he can provide (*prns*) for others from his own; of him it was said (Jer 17:7): "Blessed be the man who will trust in God, God will be his refuge."

Halakah (= Gemara):
... *dalma* (= drama, story), R. Ḥama bar Ḥanina and R. Hoshaiah were strolling in these synagogues of Lod. R. Ḥama bar Ḥanina

said to R. Hoshaiah: How much money did my ancestors invest here! He said to him: *How many souls* did your ancestors invest here? Weren't there people to labor in Torah?

R. Aḥa in the name of R. Ḥinena, thus is the Mishnah (to be recited): Everyone who should take but does not take, is a murderer (lit. spills blood) and it is prohibited to have mercy on him. On himself (*his own soul*) he takes no pity, for others how much more so?

These final sections of the eighth chapter of Mishna Pe'ah that we have cited here at length begin with the minimum allotment to an itinerant poor person who is just passing through, the poor who stays in town overnight and that poor person who stays over Shabbat. It goes on to delineate two different institutions: the *tamhui*, the common platter designed to distribute food daily to the poor and the *kupa*, the charity basket distributed weekly before Shabbat. The money is collected by a pair of collectors but was to be distributed by three people. The next Mishna defines the poverty level (200 *zuz* annually or 50 "active" *zuzim*), below which one has the right to benefit from gifts to the poor. Finally the Mishna closes by excoriating those who take charity feigning illness or the like while praising the poor person who forbears and trusts God for support rather than taking charity. This last point will be called into question in the Talmud.

The Talmud glosses these Mishnas with excerpts from the Tosefta Peah and comments by the amoraim of the Land of Israel. The first comment in the Talmud is an excerpt from the Tosefta that defines both the times of distribution of the *tamḥui* and *kupa*, while supplementing the Mishna that only specified the number of collectors of the *kupa* by doing the same for the *tamḥui*.

The amoraic discussion spends the next number of paragraphs discussing the officials who distributed charity. These officials are given the title *parnas* in the amoraic sugya, though the sugya suggests that the title existed years earlier in R. Akiva's time. This suggestion is borne out by the fact that not only does the office and its title appear in tannaitic literature such as the Tosefta and the Sifre, but epigraphic evidence supports its provenance.[13] A lead weight, deciphered by Ada Yardeni, reads, "Shim'on son of Kos[i]ba' Prince [Nasi'] of Israel and his/its *parnas*."[14] The various possibilities of the office and its title in tannaitic times have been explored by Steven Fraade. In our passage, it is clear that the *parnas* was responsible for collecting and distributing charity.

What is unique in this amoraic treatment of the *parnasim* is the conceptualization of charity within the framework of matters of life and death. I have italicized the five places in the two cited sugyot that employ phrases including *nefashot*—souls or lives. The first instance in the first sugya sets the tone for the entire passage, quite seriously placing charity on a new and dramatic plane. R. Ḥelbo in the name of R. Ba bar Zavda explains that the reasoning behind having three *parnasim* is that if monetary matters requires three judges, capital cases—here meaning charity—certainly demand three. This comment has removed charity from the category of financial dealings and placed it squarely in the category of matters of life and death—capital issues. The Talmud goes on to query—half in jest, I would suggest—well then, let's have the full quorum for a capital case—twenty-three judges. The answer is, of course, that by the time you assemble the twenty-three the poor person will be endangered.[15]

We will continue with this theme in our sugya, but we will take a short detour to point out the same theme of charity as a matter of life and death in the exquisite chapter on charity at Leviticus Rabbah 34, a midrashic collection edited in the Land of Israel soon after the Yerushalmi. In an extensive and penetrating discourse on charity, some sixty pages in the Margulies critical edition, treating Leviticus 25:35: "if your brother becomes poor," the midrash collects apposite verses from the rest of scripture to paint a stunning portrait of how and when one goes about doing *zedaka* (charity) properly. In one section, R. Pinchas in the name of R. Reuven gives poignant expression to the notion that charity is a matter of life and death. I will cite the entire paragraph leading up to and following that statement:

> "He who is generous to the poor makes a loan to God" (Prov 19:17a NJPS). Said R. Elazar, it is written, "He gives food to all flesh" (Ps 136:25 NJPS), this person came along and snatched the mitzvah, the Holy One blessed be He says "I must repay him", that is what is written: "and he will repay him his due" (Prov 19:17b). R. Tanhuma said it (in the name of) R. Ḥaggai in the name of R. Ḥiyya the Great. . . . The way of the borrower is to become a slave to the lender. R. Pinchas in the name of R. Reuven, Any one who gives a penny to the poor person, God gives him a penny. But does he give him (the poor person) just a penny? Doesn't he actually give him his life (*nafsho*)? In what way? A loaf costs ten pennies and the poor person stood to buy it but had only nine pennies in hand. One comes along and gives him a penny and he buys the loaf and eats it and his soul is restored to him. Says to him, "even you when your soul is chirping to leave your body I will restore it to you in your body." Therefore Moses warns Israel and says, "if your brother becomes poor [. . . let him live by your side]." (Lev 25:35)[16]

This is a dazzling attempt to rationalize the notion that charity is indeed a matter of life and death down to a single penny. Reason then dictates that as the charitable person has saved a life through charity, the donor's own life will be saved in return. Moreover, on a theological plane, one who aids the poor has discharged what is essentially God's duty and thus puts God in one's debt. We see then that the notion that charity is a matter of life and death, rather than mere financial magnanimity, is a concept central to the sages' outlook.

Let's return to our sugya in the Jerusalem Talmud. R. Yosi tries to persuade people in Kufra[17] to accept the position of *parnas*. He resorts to an argument based on the same notion that to be involved in charity is a matter of life and death. He reasons that if a person in the Mishna won renown for dealing with wicks in the Temple, how much more so will the *parnasim* of Kufra gain renown for dealing with the "lives of souls," *chaye nefashot*. This same unusual phrase reappears at the end of our sugya, where Rav and R. Yoḥanan are said to have debated whether we must be exacting in the distribution of clothing with one of them contending that we do scrutinize in terms of clothing but we refrain from investigating where "the lives of souls" are involved. It is R. Yosi (=Asi, Yasa) who makes this report, a third-generation amora like R. Ba bar Zavda above who employed the same term. I have not found this combination *chaye nefashot*, the life of lives, anywhere else in rabbinic literature, save the parallel to our sugya in y. Sheqalim (chapter 5).

I have skipped above a full column and a half in the best modern edition of the Jerusalem Talmud that contains wonderful anecdotes and interpretations all focusing on the importance of charity. I bring one here by way of example and in order to highlight that from the Mishna thru the amoraim, the sages were alert to the fact that sometimes people pretended to be poor. I do so to emphasize further the main point that the sages raised charity to the level of a matter of life and death.

> *Dalma* (=drama, a story) R. Yoḥanan and R. Shimon ben Lakish went to bathe in the public bath of Tiberias. A poor person met them. He said to them, "gain merit with (by) me." They said, "when we return." When they came back, they found him dead. They said, "since we did not have merit by him in his life, we will care for him in his death. While caring for him they found a pouch of dinars hanging on him. They said, "that is what R. Abbahu said that R. Elazar, 'We should be grateful to the deceivers among them for were it not for the deceivers among them if one were to demand charity from a person and did not give, he would be immediately punished.'"

These two preeminent sages of Israel were remiss, hurrying to the bath house (to keep their appointment?). In retrospect, they were spared the sin of neglecting the poor person who had accosted them (*paga* means "met," but often with a harsher tone). The bottom line is that the punishment for not responding immediately to a poor person's request for "merit" is potentially disastrous. The stakes are high. One can only surmise the effect this tale had on its audience—prompting a knee-jerk response to every beggar's plea for charity.

Another tale further on is also critical, this time of the great R. Hoshaya Rabba, who apologizes to his son's blind tutor for not dining with him, as was his custom, due to his having to entertain company. R. Hoshaya offers the following seemingly disingenuous excuse that he did not wish "to denigrate the master's honor." The tutor replies, probably sarcastically, with a bon mot that had been told to R. Elazar ben Yaakov. The story runs as follows:

> A blind person came to R. Elazar ben Yaakov's city. R. Elazar ben Yaakov sat below him,[18] they saying that were he not a great man R. Elazar would not sit below him (the blind person). They made him a very respectable gift (*parnasa*). He (the blind person) said to them, "What is this"? They said to him, "R. Elazar ben Yaakov sat below you. He (the blind person) prayed for him (R. Elazar ben Yaakov) the following prayer, "You did a deed of lovingkindness to one who is seen but does not see, the One who sees but is not seen should receive your entreaties and do lovingkindness to you."

This is a beautiful vignette, set in Greco-Roman patterns of the order of reclining, showing this sage's sensitivity to the needs of the itinerant blind person.

Toward the conclusion of this eighth chapter of Pe'ah we have been studying, which is the end of the entire tractate devoted to gifts to the poor, we find the following anecdote that follows the story of R. Elazar ben Yaakov above:

> ...*dalma* (= drama, story), R. Ḥama bar Ḥanina and R. Hoshaiah were strolling in these synagogues of Lod. R. Ḥama bar Ḥanina said to R. Hoshaiah: How much money did my ancestors sink into (invest) here! He said to him: *How many souls* did your ancestors invest here? Weren't there people to labor in Torah?

R. Ḥama seems to be taking pride in how much his ancestors had given to build and/or decorate the synagogues of Lydda.[19] R. Hoshaiah replies sharply that it would have been preferable for the money to have been invested in students of Torah, contrasting lives (*nefashot*) with edifices. R. Hoshaiah's emphasis here is on supporting students of Torah over buildings for study and prayer—literally places of assembly.[20]

The classic source for investing in people as opposed to amassing wealth is in the story of King Monabases, in the last chapter of the Tosefta Peah. Monabases, the king of Adiabene, converted to Judaism as reported both in Josephus (Antiquities 20, 2) and rabbinic sources. Josephus tells us that he opened the royal storehouses of grain and distributed it freely to the people in a time of famine. The Tosefta reports that this rankled his brothers who charged, "Your ancestors stored away treasures and added to that of their ancestors, but you stood and wasted (distributed) all your storehouses, yours and your ancestors." Monabases, according to the Tosefta, gives a number of replies, of which we will quote but two: "My ancestors stored below, but I stored above... my ancestors stored money, but I stored lives, as it says, 'the fruit of the righteous is a tree of life; a wise man acquires souls (*nefashot*)' (Prov. 11, 30)" (t. Pe'ah 4:18).[21] Fine essays[22] have traced the phrase "treasures in heaven," especially with reference to charity, as it appears prominently in the Sermon on the Mount, Matthew 6:19–21:

Do not lay up for yourselves treasures on earth where moth and rust destroy, where thieves break in and steal, but lay up for yourselves treasures in heaven.... For where your treasure us, there your heart will be...

For our purpose, the tradition in the Tosefta pits charity, which impacts lives, against amassing wealth (*nefashot/mammon*), which is the exact motif that runs through the sugya in the Jerusalem Talmud.

The finale of this long and intense exploration of charity in the Jerusalem Talmud Peah chapter 8, of which we have brought a small selection, is a remarkable and bold correction of the Mishna's stance by an amora. The Mishna 8:9 praises those who put their trust in God and refrain from taking charity, even though they are in need. The Mishna states that they will eventually be blessed by God with the ability to help others. To this the amora R. Aḥa in the name of Rabbi Ḥinena objects vehemently saying, "this is the way the Mishna should read— "Everyone who should take but does not take, is a murderer (lit. spills blood) and it is prohibited to have mercy on him. On himself (*his own soul*) he takes no pity, for others how much more so?" Abstaining from needed charity shows a callousness to the plight of one's own life (*nafshe*), a sure indication that this person will not be merciful to others.

We have tried to show that the leitmotif in this Jerusalem Talmud is charity as a matter of life and death. Now this notion possibly has its roots in Proverbs 11:30, "the fruit of the righteous is a tree of life; a wise man acquires souls (*nefashot*)," and is adumbrated in the putatively first-century Monabases story in the Tosefta. But there is no question that the Jerusalem Talmud has moved charity to a new level of intensity. Was this due to the dire economic and political conditions that plagued the Roman Empire in what is called "the third century crisis," with its twenty emperors and rampant inflation? R. Yoḥanan, who died in Tiberias in 279 CE, is cited in the Babylonian Talmud, as one who recalled people bloated by hunger in Tiberias not due to a lack of food but to poverty (b. Ta'anit 19b, b. Bava Batra 91b). It may very well be that the economic crisis gave charity a greater urgency than ever before. Both the y. Pe'ah passages we have treated and the Leviticus Rabbah midrashic chapter 34 on charity reflect a strong feeling that charity is a matter of life and death for the poor.

This is a unique approach to charity. But, as hinted to above in the reluctance of people to act as *parnas*, the distribution of charity and especially the criteria for prioritization, demanded sensitivity. On the whole from the Mishna Horayot 3, 7, and on, males in general and learned males in particular, were given priority in matters of life and death—a male is rescued from death according to the Mishna before a female. Even the literary structure of that Mishna begins and ends with the same statement: "The males precedes the female", a blatantly patriarchal turn. That same Mishna does however accord women priority in being given clothing, and the Talmud,[23] at least according to some interpreters, includes women's priority for being fed.

The application of the rules in Mishna and Tosefta Horayot, along with their elaboration in Jerusalem Talmud and Babylonian Talmud, would seem to indicate that the rules of distribution made a clear distinction between saving a life and giving charity. This would lead us to the conclusion that the theme developed in the Jerusalem Talmud Peah and Midrash Leviticus Rabbah was designed essentially to increase the moral suasion on the givers, impressing upon them that giving charity can be a matter of life and death.

References

Albeck, Chanoch (1957), *Seder Zeraim* (Jerusalem and Tel Aviv: Bialik Institute and Dvir).
Anderson, Gary A. (2013), *Charity: The Place of the Poor in the Biblical Tradition* (New Haven, CT: Yale University Press).

Brown, Peter (2002), *Poverty and Leadership in the Later Roman Empire* (Hanover: University Press of New England).

Fraade, Steven D. (2011), *Legal Fictions: Studies of Law and Narrative in the Discursive Worlds of Ancient Jewish Sectarians and Sages* (Leiden: Brill) (= Fraade, Steven D. (2011), "Local Jewish Leadership in Roman Palestine: The Case of the Parnas in Early Rabbinic Sources in Light of Extra Rabbinic Evidence," in Albert I Baumgarten et al. (eds.), *Halakah in Light of Epigraphy* (Göttingen: Vandenhoeck &Ruprecht): 157–175).

Gardner, Gregg E. (2022), *Wealth, Poverty and Charity in Jewish Antiquity* (Oakland: University of California Press).

Gorzalczany, Amir, Avissar, M., Torgë, H., ʿAd, U., Jakoel, E. and Elisha, Y. (2016), "Lod, The Lod Mosaic," *Hadashot Arkheologiyot: Excavations and Surveys in Israel* 128, https://www.jstor.org/stable/26678944.

Gray, Alyssa M. (2019), *Charity in Rabbinic Judaism: Atonement, Rewards, and Righteousness* (New York and London: Routledge).

Greenwood, David Neal (2021), *Julian and Christianity: Revisiting the Constantinian Revolution* (Ithaca, NY: Cornell University Press).

Julian (1923), *Letters. Epigrams. Against the Galilaeans. Fragments* (Wilmer C. Wright, trans.); LCL 157 (Cambridge, MA: Harvard University Press).

Margulies, Mordecai, ed. (1993), *Leviticus Rabbah* (2 vols.) (Hebrew) (New York: The Jewish Theological Seminary).

Meir, Daniel (2007), "The Parnas in Israel—Identity, Status and Authority," (Hebrew) M.A thesis, The Hebrew University of Jerusalem.

Novick, Tzvi (2012), "Charity and Reciprocity: Structures of Benevolence in Rabbinic Literature," *Harvard Theological Review* 105: 33–52, http://www.jstor.org/stable/41474562.

Satlow, Michael L. (2010), "'Fruit and the Fruit of Fruit': Charity and Piety among Jews in Late Antique Palestine," *Jewish Quarterly Review* 100: 244–277, http://www.jstor.org/stable/20750702.

Schwartz, Seth (2010), *Were the Jews a Mediterranean Society? Reciprocity and Solidarity in Ancient Judaism* (Princeton, NJ: Princeton University Press).

Sokoloff, Michael (1990), *A Dictionary of Jewish Palestinian Aramaic of the Byzantine Period* (Ramat Gan: Bar-Ilan University Press).

Stern, Menahem (1974), *Greek and Latin Authors on Jews and Judaism* (3 vols.) (Jerusalem: Israel Academy of Sciences and Humanities).

Urbach, Ephraim E. (1951), "Political and Social Tendencies in Talmudic Concepts of Charity" (Hebrew), *Zion* 16: 1–27, https://www.jstor.org/stable/23548465. Reprinted in Urbach, Ephraim E. (1988), *The World of the Sages: Collected Studies* (Jerusalem: Magnes Press): 97–124.

Urbach, Ephraim E. (1980), "Treasures Above," in Gérard Nahon et al. (eds.), *Hommage à George Vajda* (Louvain: Editions Peeters): 117–124. Reprinted in Urbach, Ephraim E. (1999), *Collected Writings in Jewish Studies* (Jerusalem: Magnes Press): 281–288.

Weinfeld, Moshe (1995), *Social Justice in Ancient Israel and in the Ancient Near East* (Minneapolis: Fortress Press; Jerusalem: Magnes Press).

Wilfand Ben Shalom, Yael (2014), *Poverty, Charity and the Image of the Poor in Rabbinic Texts from the Land of Israel* (Sheffield: Sheffield Phoenix Press).

Wilfand Ben Shalom, Yael (2017), *The Wheel That Overtakes Everyone: Poverty and Charity in the Eyes of the Sages of the Land of Israel* (Hebrew) (Tel Aviv: Hakibbutz Hameuchad).

4
Love and Passion
Between Earth and Heaven

In this chapter, I hope to break new ground in analyzing an extraordinary treatment of love in the great fifth-century Midrash Genesis Rabbah, after canvassing some of the more familiar presentations in rabbinic literature and early Christian literature. The centrality of love in their respective religions, is attributed to great religious figures in both early Christianity and rabbinic Judasim. There are different kinds of love, as the Midrash on Song of Songs pointed out, from filial love to erotic love. Here we will highlight one aspect of religious erotic love.

Within the five books of Moses, love of and reverence for God were given pride of place in Deuteronomy's religious view (Lapsley 2003). It was love of God that became the theme song of the average Jew's everyday existence. Sometime in Second Temple times, the recitation of Deuteronomy 6:5 with its command to love God wholeheartedly, with one's entire soul and might (lit. "very-ness"), became the central ritual in Jewish life and quite likely in the Jerusalem Temple as well (m. Tamid 4:1). As opposed to the Temple, where there was no official nighttime activity, the individual Jew and the community service both began their day with the injunction to love God and repeated the same at night. As noted above, love of God and one's fellow human were central to the religious view of the great R. Akiva, who accorded to the Song of Songs the holiest place in Scripture and called it "the holy of holies." The same R. Akiva saw loving one's neighbor as the great principle of the Torah.[1]

The New Testament, in the gospel of Mark 12, quotes Jesus, after being queried what is the primary commandment *(entole prote)*, as responding with love of God first and love of neighbor second. Yet it is to be noted well that the passage in Mark begins not with the commandment of love but with the preceding verse, "Hear O Israel the Lord our God the Lord is one"—the first verse of Shema, the Deuteronomy passages that evidently shaped the Jew's everyday life in Jesus's time, at least according to Mark's report decades later (12:28–30). The parallel passage in Matthew 22:37 begins directly with the commandment to love, omitting the credo.

Paul waxes eloquent over the virtues and importance of love (1 Cor 13:1–8):

> If I speak in the tongues of men or of angels, but do not have love, I am only a resounding gong or a clanging cymbal. If I have the gift of prophecy and can fathom all mysteries and all knowledge, and if I have a faith that can move mountains, but do not have love, I am nothing. If I give all I possess to the poor and give over my body to hardship that I may boast, but do not have love, I gain nothing. Love is patient, love is kind. It does not envy, it does not boast, it is not proud. It does not dishonor others, it is not self-seeking, it is not easily angered, it keeps no record of wrongs, does not delight in evil but rejoices with the truth. It always protects, always trusts, always hopes, always perseveres. Love never fails...

It is curious, then, that the New Testament never directly cites the greatest of biblical love songs, the Song of Songs, at all. How can we explain this apparent anomaly? Peter Tomson, in an ingenious reading of some New Testament passages on the bridegroom and the fig tree,[2] attempts to locate allusions to verses in the Song of Songs, with some degree of success. But I find J. Winanady's conclusion, that in the eyes of the New Testament the Song of Songs did not have the same meanings that were developed by the later Fathers of the church, more convincing.[3] Tomson himself addresses the question as to why, then, is there no direct citation of the Song in the New Testament. His tentative answer was the "ambiguous" canonical status of the work.[4] But surely, in a collection of sacred writings spanning over a century, with two of the great protagonists, Jesus and Paul, proclaiming love as the cardinal virtue, one would have expected a more direct reliance on the Song. Was early Christianity deliberately shunning the eroticism of the Song? Only the great Christian Bible scholar and philosopher, Origen of Alexandria and later of Caesarea, would, in dialogue with his Jewish teachers, find the answer to integrating fully this erotic work into Christian theology.

It was, then, the church father Origen, in his third-century homilies and commentary on the Song of Songs, who gave full expression to love of God, referring to and deepening the classic Greek distinction between *eros* and *agape*. Agape was the term for the more ethereal, spiritual love, but Origen insisted in his acute reading of Scripture that when it comes to love of divine wisdom, Scripture uses the earthier *eros* to describe it:

> Occasionally, however, though rarely it calls the passion of love by its own name, and invites and urges souls to it, as when it says in Proverbs about Wisdom: Desire her greatly...[5]

All of the above has been the object of intense scholarly research. The most recent and penetrating analysis of this theme in terms of teacher–pupil in Origen's own school is to be found in David Satran's recent monograph, *In the Image of Origen: Eros, Virtue and Restraint in the Early Christian Academy*. He quotes Origen's student Gregory in his farewell discourse as follows:

Like a spark landed in the midst of our soul, the love (*eros*) for the most attractive Word (*Logos*), holy and most desired in its unspeakable beauty, and for this man [Origen] who is its friend, was kindled and inflamed (6.83).[6]

We will turn our attention to the nature of love, or better the language of love, beginning with a surprising, even disconcerting homily, attributed to the famous Simon ben Lakish.

I begin then, not without great hesitancy, with the disturbing comment by the great third-century Palestinian sage R. Simon ben Lakish. But before we study his comment, we will delve into the biography of this famous scholar who studied and debated with R. Yohanan, the doyen of Land of Israel amoraim. Simon ben Lakish has entered the modern and postmodern Jewish consciousness due to a tale spun in b. Bava Metzi'a, in a sugya that, to me and some other students of rabbinic literature, seems to go out of its way to cast a negative light on Land of Israel sages.[7] The first set of tales in the sugya portraying R. Elazar, the son of Simon ben Yohai, was characterized by one recent scholar as evincing "the cultural dynamics of a talmudic text in which the thematics of the grotesque are obsessively present, as in Rabelais."[8]

Who was R. Simon ben Lakish, better known by the nickname Reish Lakish, given him in Babylonian Talmud and less pristine manuscripts and editions of Land of Israel texts?[9] Bacher surmises that he might have been a student of Bar Kappara in the south, since he often quotes teachings of Bar Kappara.[10] What seems clear from the Jerusalem Talmud is that he resorted to physical prowess to right wrongs done to people (y. Terumot 8:9 46c) and even danced for his wine according to a Land of Israel midrash (Qohelet Rabbah 10:16). The Babylonian tradition that he was a brigand and/or gladiator is unknown in Land of Israel sources,[11] though R. Simon does make reference once to a *bon mot* that speaks of "ludarios," one who participated in the circus or games. Of paramount importance is the fact that R. Berechia calls him and his study partner/

teacher, R. Yoḥanan, "the greats of the world" (y. Berachot 8:6, 12c). Bacher attributes to R. Simon ben Lakish a penchant for daring homilies,[12] in some of them raising radical views about God. Let us look at his description of God's love for Israel.

> "And Hamor spoke with them saying" (Gen 34:8). Said R. Simon ben Lakish, With three expressions of affection (*ḥiba*) the Holy One blessed be He loved (*ḥibb*) Israel, with clinging (*dbk*), with lusting (*ḥsk*) and with desiring (*ḥfz*). With clinging, "and you cling to God" (Deut 4:4); with lusting, "It is not because you are the most numerous of peoples that the Lord set his heart (*ḥsk*) on you" (Deut 7:7); with desiring, "and all the nations shall account you happy for you shall be the most desired (*ḥfz*) of lands" (Mal 3:12). (Gen. Rab. 80:8)

R. Simon ben Lakish has focused on God's erotic love for Israel. This becomes quite clear in the continuation of this same homily:

> And we learn all three from the biblical section of this villain, "and she (his soul) clinged" (Gen 34:3), here is clinging, with lusting, "his soul lusted" (Gen 34:8), with desiring, "for he desired the daughter of Jacob (Gen 34:19).

Why in the world would the great R. Simon ben Lakish describe God's love for Israel with erotic terms drawn from the painful story of the rape of Dinah at Genesis 34? This question is even more striking when one continues on to the subsequent homily, of R. Abba ben Elyashiv, who quickly adds two more words mentioned in the same story, the one so glaringly omitted by R. Simon ben Lakish—love (*ahv*)!

Before grappling with this difficult passage, we should note, as Julius Theodor did in his magnificent edition of Genesis Rabbah, that R. Simon ben Lakish has another homily, structured in the same way later on in Genesis Rabbah 90:2. There he begins, "Two things Moses gave us in the Torah and we learn them from the biblical section of the villain." In that case, R. Simon ben Lakish focuses on issues of power. He opines that just as Pharaoh twice elevates Joseph but quickly adds that Pharaoh's own power and throne are supreme, so, too, Israel's greatness and holiness are secondary to God's own greatness and holiness. Comprehending power relations between God the king and God's people Israel by comparison to Pharaoh is not so different from the oft-used king parables in rabbinic literature. Though this homily of R. Simon ben Lakish on power and our homily on affection share an identical rhetorical opening, it hardly explains the egregious nature of comparing God's love of Israel to the terms found in the rape of Dinah.

As was to be expected, the great sixteenth-century commentator on midrash, R. Shmuel Yaffe Ashkenazi, raised this very question and went to great lengths to explain this perplexing homily in his massive commentary on Genesis Rabbah, the *Yefe Toar*.[13] We quote an excerpt from the commentary in my own translation:

> And moreover, what does God's holy love have to do with this despicable love that we learn from it, "Who can make a pure thing from an impure one . . ." (Job 14: 4)? I found that it is only possible to estimate spiritual love by comparison with physical love, as Seneca wrote. Therefore, to comprehend the extent of God's love for Israel, it was compared to the love of a good desirer (*hoshek*) to his good object of desire. For a good desirer will first desire a bit the object of his desire, but after that will desire her and no other, and then will cling to her and it is his life, so are we with God.

The *Yefe Toar* cites Solomon's Song of Songs as another instance of comparing human love to God and Israel's mutual love. But despite that, R. Simon ben Lakish's analogy to what is later called the rape of Dinah remains "a great question without a remedy." The commentator goes on to spend a few pages developing a typology of three kinds of love. He demonstrates how this homily uniquely captures them and why they are appropriate in describing God's love.

The focus of our own interpretation will be R. Simon's omission of the word *love*, *ahava*, which, as R. Abba pointed out, also appears in the Dinah episode. It might be that, in a vein similar to Origen above, R. Simon ben Lakish is targeting erotic love as a (the?) constituent element of God's love for Israel and Israel's love of God. He begins by distancing himself from the villain of the rape of Dinah, by calling him out as a villain, as R. Simon did also in his homily on Pharaoh and power. Yet this famous sage chooses to emphasize erotic love, drawing a parallel between the language used to describe Shehem's attack on and subsequent attraction to Dinah, to two of Deuteronomy's characterizations of God's love for Israel, *ḥsk*, and Israel's clinging, *dbk*, to God. The third language of love is the less charged verb *ḥfz* (desire), taken from Malachi. On two occasions then, R. Simon ben Lakish likened royal power and human eros to divine power and eros between the divine and Israel, respectively.

Left to my own imagination, I might say that what R. Simon is advocating is a very earthy love. This conception of Israel and God's relationship eschews the ethereal and intangible. It is an earthy, religious stance, easily grasped by the audience. But is this what R. Simon ben Lakish meant? Probably not. We have to pay close attention to the fact that the two words that are most erotic *ḥsk* (lust) and *dbk* (cling) explicitly state that it was Shehem's soul[14] that clinged and lusted. I suggest that R. Simon ben Lakish has harnessed the vocabulary of eros to the soul's yearning. It then very much serves as a paradigm for love of God and God's love of Israel. Or as the Sifre Deut (49) glossed the verse "to cling to Him" (Deut 11:22):

> Can a person possibly ascend to heaven and cling to fire—Hasn't it been said, "For your Lord God is a consuming fire" (Deut 4:24).

R. Simon has adroitly linked the fiery passion of erotic love of the soul with the love of God. How does R. Simon ben Lakish's view of eros relate to some rabbinic views of the *yezer hara*, "the evil inclination"? The eros as depicted by R. Simon ben Lakish accords well to those who saw the *yezer hara* as a positive motivating factor. It is worth quoting Ishay Rosen-Zvi's treatment of an important source for the evil inclination at length:

> This is the case, for example, with the famous homily in Genesis Rabbah 9:7 (ed. Theodor-Albeck, 72):
>
> Behold, it was very good (Gen 1:31): refers to the good yetzer; and behold . . . it was very good (idem): refers to the evil yetzer. But is evil yetzer good . . . ? Rather, without the evil yetzer no man would build a house, take a wife or beget children and thus Solomon says: [I have also noted that all labor and skillful enterprise] come from man's rivalry with his neighbor (Eccl 4:4).
>
> Daniel Boyarin comments on this homily: "Sexuality according to them is neither in itself evil (as apparently many first-century Jews held), nor is it an uncomplicated good, despite the fact that it leads to building the houses, marrying, procreation and eggs! It is called the Evil Instinct solely because of its destructive side." Other scholars similarly infer from this homily: "Sexuality, nevertheless, is good." But does "yetzer" here refer solely or even primarily to sexuality? I suspect not. True, the yetzer *appears here as an Eros-like figure, but only in the most general sense of a creative drive or force* (my emphasis). The homily quotes a verse that explicitly states that envy and competition are the issues at hand, and while they may lead to marriage and procreation, they are also the source of "all labor and skillful enterprise" (Eccl 4:4). The appearance of envy as a product of the yetzer should not surprise us, for similar descriptions appear with regard to other dangerous passions and moods such as anger and pride.[15]

Let's return now to the first part of R. Simon ben Lakish's bold homily. It begins "With three expressions of affection (*ḥiba*) the Holy One blessed be He loved (*ḥibb*) Israel." I want to focus on *ḥiba* in rabbinic literature, here translated as "affection." David Stern devoted an essay to the first chapter of Leviticus Rabbah, which develops the theme of prophecy and the uniqueness of Moses's relationship with God. In that chapter, the midrash employs the term *ḥavivut* in three of the fourteen sections of the chapter. Stern remarks: "By joining havivut with midrash, a new religious language was created whose very purpose was to reinvoke God as a familiar and intimate presence."[16] There is no question that the root *ḥbb* evokes intimacy and familiarity. Given our findings above, that R. Simon ben Lakish saw three erotic terms as language of *ḥiba*, we need give renewed attention to the vocabulary of love in rabbinic literature.

The root *ḥbb* appears only once in Scripture, in the *qal* form, at Deuteronomy 33:3.[17] The Septuagint there translates it with the aorist form (*epheisato*) of a Greek word (*pheidomai*) that means "to spare or have mercy." But the Hebrew *piel* form is in frequent use in rabbinic literature, as instanced above, and has a range of meanings from love, endear, and favor, to the more erotic tinge we saw in R. Simon's words. R. Akiva invoked the term when he declared what should be construed as his fundamental religious view:

> Beloved (*ḥaviv*) is the human (*adam*) who was created in the image [of God]. Especially beloved (*ḥiba*) since it was made known to him that he had been created in the image [of God], as it is said: "for in the image of God He made man" (Gen 9:6).
>
> Beloved (*ḥaviv*) are Israel in that they were named children of the All-Present. Especially beloved are they for it was made known to them that they were named children of the All-Present, as it is said: "you are children to the Lord your God" (Deut 14:1).
>
> Beloved (*ḥaviv*) are Israel in that an instrument was given to them. Especially beloved are they for it was made known to them

that the instrument, with which the world had been created, was given to them, as it is said: "for I give you good instruction; forsake not my teaching" (Prov 4:2). (m. Avot 3:14)

What then was love of God for the rabbis? On the basis of the source above, I would characterize it as the fiery love of passion. Elie Wiesel aptly titled one of his books *Souls on Fire*. This was to be an all-consuming love,[18] and stories are told of rabbis so immersed in love of God and Torah that they lost their way and even unwittingly violated Sabbath boundaries or were oblivious to their own apparel.[19] The verse that captured this all-encompassing love, in addition to Deuteronomy 6:2—with all your heart, soul and might—was Proverbs 5:19: "A loving doe . . . Let her breasts satisfy you at all times, Be infatuated with love of her always." The verb translated here as "infatuated" (*tishge*), is more literally translated as "go astray." The verse appears at y. Berachot 5:1, 9a, where two Land of Israel amoraim are so engrossed in their study that they are oblivious to what is going on around them. The object of love here, as in Proverbs, is Wisdom or for the rabbis, Torah.[20] In that sense, the rabbinic sages might be called philosophers, lovers of wisdom (*philo-sophia*). Their wisdom was Torah. The real object of love in the rabbinic world was love of Torah.[21] In the words the midrash attributed to the Tanna Rabbi Nathan: "Rabbi Nathan says, 'There is no love like the love of Torah; There is no wisdom like the wisdom of the land of Israel'" (Avot of Rabbi Nathan version A, chapter 28).[22]

This loving devotion to Torah began in Second Temple times—Psalms 119:97: "How I love your Torah, Lord! All day long it is my study/talk/meditation."[23] The love of Torah was the centerpiece of rabbinic ritual for the morning and evening prayers, reciting the blessing of God's love for Israel as the lead in to the "reading" of Deuteronomy 6:4ff, the Shema. This benediction celebrates God's eternal love for Israel that was evidenced by their receiving the Torah and commandments. Though there was a special blessing to be recited before any study of Torah, this daily blessing preceding the Shema was considered its equivalent and rightly so. According to one rabbinic view (b. Menahot 99b), recitation of Shema in the morning and the evening basically fulfilled the command "Let not this Book of Torah cease from your lips, but recite it day and night" (Jo 1:8). In a way, the commandment to love God in the Shema was best carried out by loving God's Torah.

This is so much the case that the great third-century Babylonian sage Rav, founder of the Sura academy, added a personal prayer after the eighteen benedictions wherein he prayed for "a life of love of Torah and fear of Heaven" (b. Berakhot 16b). That great conundrum of what was preferable, the love of God or fear of God, was elegantly resolved by Rav. Fear or respect God, but love God's Torah.

We will conclude this chapter by recalling R Akiva's bold statement that "Song of Songs is the holy of holies." This stance resonates in a Babylonian amora's statement about the holy of holies:

> Said Rav Katina, When Israel would come up for pilgrimage they would roll up the covering (*parochet*) and show the cherubim intertwined with one another and say to them, "See your belovedness (*ḥiba*) before God (*hamakom*) is as the love of a male with a female."

This stunning picture brings us full circle to our Land of Israel amora, R. Simon ben Lakish. Earthy erotic love was perceived by him and by his contemporary Rav Katina in Babylonia, as reflecting God's passion for Israel. Heavenly love and earthly passion were not inimical.[24]

References

Bacher, Wilhelm (1892; reprint 1965), *Die Aggada der palästinensischen Amoräer* (Strassburg: Trübner).

Benayahu, Meir (1973), "R. Samuel Yaffe Ashkenazi and Other Commentators of 'Midrash Rabba,'" *Tarbiz* 42: 419–460, https://www.jstor.org/stable/23593547.

Boyarin, Daniel (1995), *Carnal Israel: Reading Sex in Talmudic Culture* (Berkeley: The University of California Press).

Fishbane, Michael (1996), *The Kiss of God: Spiritual and Mystical Death in Judaism* (Seattle: University of Washington Press).

Idel, Moshe (2005), *Kabbalah and Eros* (New Haven, CT: Yale University Press).

Lapsley, Jacqueline E. (2003), "Feeling Our Way: Love for God in Deuteronomy," *The Catholic Biblical Quarterly* 65: 350–369, http://www.jstor.org/stable/43725006.

Lawson, R. P. (1957), *Origen: The Song of Songs Commentary and Homilies* (Westminster: The Newman Press).

Levenson, Jon D. (2016), *The Love of God: Divine Gift, Human Gratitude, and Mutual Faithfulness in Judaism* (Princeton, NJ: Princeton University Press).

Rosen-Zvi, Ishay (2011), *Demonic Desires: Yetzer Hara and the Problem of Evil in Late Antiquity* (Philadelphia: University of Pennsylvania Press), www.upenn.edu/pennpress.

Satran, David (2018), *In the Image of Origen: Eros, Virtue, and Constraint in the Early Christian Academy* (Oakland: University of California Press).

Stern, David (1986), "Midrash and the Language of Exegesis: A Study of Vayikra Rabbah, Chapter 1," in *Midrash and Literature* (New Haven, CT: Yale University Press): 105–124.

Tomson, Peter J. (2015), "The Song of Songs in the Teachings of Jesus and the Development of the Exposition on the Song," *New Testament Studies* 61, no. 4: 429–447.

Uusimäki, Elisa (2014), "'Happy Is the Person to Whom She Has Been Given': The Continuum of Wisdom and Torah in 4Q Sapiential Admonitions B (4Q185) and 4QBeatitudes (4Q525)," *Revue de Qumran* 26: 345–359, https://www.jstor.org/stable/24663196.

Wasserstein, Abraham (1979), "A Good Man Fallen among Robbers," *Tarbiz* 49: 197–198, https://www.jstor.org/stable/23595082.

Winandy, Jacques (1964), "Le Cantique des Cantiques et le Nouveau Testament," *Revue Biblique* 71, no. 2: 161–190, http://www.jstor.org/stable/44089642.

5
Philosophy in Rabbinic Circles
More Than Meets the Eye?

We will treat these two disparate but related subjects, philosophy and mysticism, in separate chapters, viewing them both through the towering figure of Rabban Yoḥanan ben Zakkai. While the Tosefta Ḥagiga 2:2 casts him as the founder of a mystic chain of tradition, explicit statements concerning his philosophic inclinations are not in evidence. But, in a provocative and stimulating article, Judah Goldin first raised the possibility, with some diffidence,[1] that Rabban Yoḥanan led a philosophic session in his Beit Midrash. Let us begin with a brief survey of scholarly opinion on philosophy in late antique rabbinic literature.

One of the most formative and influential academic essays I read while still an undergraduate was by Harry Austryn Wolfson, the great early twentieth-century student of philosophy, "The Double Faith Theory in Clement, Saadia, Averroes and St. Thomas, and Its Origin in Aristotle and the Stoics."[2] Wolfson surveys and analyzes the medieval attitudes toward the relationship of faith to reason. Saadia and many great rabbis of the Middle Ages sought to reconcile the oral and written Torah with the philosophic tradition. This tradition was mediated through the Arabic sources. Though late antique rabbinic literature often employs the Hebraized form of "*philosophos*," and in the Mishna itself the rabbis as a group are called *ḥahamim* (= *sophoi*), there is precious little mention or engagement with philosophic doctrines. Rabbinic sources shun mentioning by name any of the renowned philosophers save Epicurus and one Oenomaus (=Abnimos), a second-century local Gadarene Cynic philosopher living not far from the Sea of Galilee.[3] Were the Jewish sages conversant with the philosophic tradition? This is not a new question. Warren Zev Harvey revisited the question and quoted earlier views of Harry Austryn Wolfson and Saul Lieberman, the preeminent twentieth-century Talmudist, who noted that Greek philosophical terms were not to be found in rabbinic literature.[4] Most recently, Richard Hidary has summarized the state of this question within the context of the overall contact of the cultures in a fine essay on "The Greco-Roman West and Rabbinic Literature in Palestine and Babylonia."[5]

We will again begin with Rabban Yoḥanan ben Zakkai and his students. It was Judah Goldin who boldly suggested that we can see in the following source from Avot "A Philosophical Session in a Tannaite Academy."[6]

We read at Avot 2:8–9:

> Rabban Yoḥanan ben Zakkai received from Hillel and Shammai.
>
> He used to say: if you have done/learned[7] much Torah, do not think "good of yourself" (*taḥazik tova leatzmach*),[8] because for this were you created.
>
> Rabban Yoḥanan ben Zakkai had five disciples and they were these: R. Eliezer ben Hyrcanus, R. Joshua ben Ḥananiah, R. Yose, the priest, R. Simon ben Nethanel and R. Elazar ben Arach.
>
> He used to repeat their praise: R. Eliezer ben Hyrcanus—a plastered cistern that loses not a drop; R. Joshua ben Ḥananiah— happy is the woman that gave birth to him; R. Yose the priest— a pious man; R. Simon ben Nethanel—one that fears sin, and R. Elazar ben Arach—a spring that surges.
>
> He used to say: if all the sages of Israel were on one pan of the balance scale and R. Eliezer ben Hyrcanus on the other pan, he would outweigh them all. Abba Shaul said in his name: if all the sages of Israel were on one pan of the balance scale, and

R. Eliezer ben Hyrcanus also with them, and R. Elazar ben Arach on the other pan, he would outweigh them all.

He said to them: go out and see which is the good way to which a man should adhere?

R. Eliezer said, a good eye; R. Joshua said, a good companion; R. Yose said, a good neighbor; R. Simon said, one who sees consequences (lit. that which is born). R. Elazar said, a good heart. He said to them: I see the words of Elazar ben Arach, for in his words your words are included.

He said to them: go out and see which is the evil way that a man should shun? R. Eliezer said, an evil eye; R. Joshua said, an evil companion; R. Yose said, an evil neighbor; R. Simon said, one who borrows and does not repay, for he that borrows from man is as one who borrows from God, blessed be He, as it is said, "the wicked borrow and do not repay, but the righteous deal graciously and give" (Ps 37:21). R. Elazar said, an evil heart. He said to them: I see the words of Elazar ben Arach, for in his words your words are included.[9]

In a provocative and elegant essay, Goldin points out that though Rabban Yoḥanan sees doing or studying Torah as the reason for a person's creation, none of his students mention Torah in their replies to their teacher as to what is the good path. Goldin also shows that the format of posing a question in positive form and then in the negative is a common feature of Stoic philosophy. Goldin quotes A. D. Nock as emphasizing along with others that philosophy in the Roman Empire focused on ethics. Finally, Goldin emphasizes that Rabban Yoḥanan's favored student, R. Elazar ben Arach, goes on in the same chapter of Avot to state (according to the better manuscript versions), "Be diligent to learn what to respond to the Epicurean." Goldin opens his essay by saying that there is ample evidence for legal and aggadic sessions, and as we noted above and will study in our next chapter, mystical sessions. The Avot source raises the possibility for Goldin that there might have been also sessions devoted to philosophy. It is therefore natural, Goldin answers his own question, that Rabban Yoḥanan's students refrain from answering with Torah but respond with ethical traits. Goldin's essay, bolstered by fine linguistic points and rich parallels from Greek authors, remains as stimulating and provocative as it was when it appeared, almost sixty years ago.

I will admit that I find Goldin's hypothesis convincing. His is a modest claim that there were sessions devoted to ethical issues, not to the exclusion of the predominant legal and aggadic sessions. He emphasized at the outset that he was certain that the rabbis "were not Platos in Hebrew disguise."[10] I hope to further his suggestion with the following comments and interpretations.

The question Rabban Yoḥanan posed to his students was, "Go and see, which is the good[11] way (*derech tova*) to which a person (*adam*) should cleave?" The "good way" or "good path" is a biblical phrase appearing a handful of times in Samuel, Kings (Solomon's prayer), Jeremiah, and elsewhere.[12] In 1 Samuel 12:23, Samuel declares that he will continue to instruct Israel "the good and right way." Rabban Yoḥanan chose to formulate the question "good way" as opposed to the later formulation of R. Judah the Patriarch who posed the same question over a century later. R. Judah's is the first Mishna that leads off this same chapter two of Avot, but R. Judah the patriarch uses the other term, "which is the right way (*derech yeshara*)."[13] It appears that Rabban Yoḥanan here is echoing the verse from Jeremiah 6:16: "Thus says the Lord: Stand by the roads, and look, and ask for the ancient paths, where the good way (*derech hatov*) is; and walk in it, and find rest for your souls." Rabban Yoḥanan indeed asks but replaces the "stand" of Jeremiah with "go out." "What is the good path" is definitely a philosophical question, but as we see, it has its antecedent in the Bible itself. Indeed, the topic of "the good" is lightly adumbrated in Rabban Yoḥanan's opening statement—urging a person not to hold to one's credit (*tova*) having done or studied much Torah. It is therefore unremarkable that four of the five students answer the question of the good path, by invoking "good" as an adjective describing something else—good eye, good friend, good neighbor, and good heart and their opposites for the bad path. Only Simon ben Netanel strikes a different note, ignoring the word *good* in his reply. This student who was characterized by his teacher as "fearing sin" emphasized accordingly the need for foresight and repaying a debt, the latter a commonplace of Greek philosophy at least as far back as Simonides in Plato's Republic (1 331d-e), as Goldin pointed out.[14] Simon ben Netanel is on the lookout to avoid sin and stresses the trait of watchfulness as being the good.

I have tried to give the biblical background to Rabban Yoḥanan's questions in order to highlight the fact that the quest for the good pervades Near Eastern wisdom culture and is both independent of and antecedent to Greek philosophy. I do so only to reiterate that the evidence Goldin mustered—the form of Rabban Yoḥanan's questioning, the nature of the answers, and R. Elazar's injunction to be diligent to know what to reply to the Epicurean—goes pretty far to establish his case that this is indeed a philosophical session. What, though, is missing?

Missing is the systematic argumentation that characterizes the philosophic mode. As a younger contemporary of Rabban Yoḥanan, the great Stoic philosopher Epictetus wrote:

> Behold the beginning of Philosophy!—a recognition of the conflict of the opinions of men, and a search (*zetesis*) for the origin of the conflict, and a condemnation of mere opinion, coupled with skepticism regarding it and a kind of investigation to determine whether the opinion is rightly held, together with the invention of a kind of standard of judgement.[15]

Epictetus goes on to claim rhetorically that even this is not quite enough, but it suffices to highlight for us the difficulty in seeing this tantalizing remnant of a tannaitic "philosophic session" as indeed philosophy. It is definitely ethics and, as Goldin asserted, ethics was the focus of late antique philosophy, but without the attendant argumentation, it is at best the summary or the beginning of a philosophic session.

So, too, when Warren Zev Harvey, arguing that there was indeed philosophizing in the rabbinic sphere, adducing the Talmudic passage that the House of Shammai and the House of Hillel debated for two and a half years whether it is good that a person be born, asserts:

> The Talmud, it is true, reports the debate in only four short lines, but surely in the course of two and a half years a great deal more ... must have been said by the schools of Hillel and Shammai on this basic existential question which had also occupied the Greek philosophers. We may imagine that among all that was said in those two and a half years, there were at least some rational or philosophic arguments.[16]

Yes, the Talmud is certainly a vast repository of rational arguments, but the debate and argumentation are of a legal nature or scriptural hermeneutics, rather than philosophical.[17] Now, as Goldin pointed out, the passage in Avot quoted above is already exceptional in describing a dialogue, otherwise missing in Mishna Avot, itself a collection of wise sayings and apothegms. Exceptional also is Rabban Yoḥanan's explaining his preference for the "good heart"—as all the other traits are subsumed under it. Even in the legal dicta of the Mishna, argumentation is the exception,[18] recording debates for the most part without the reasoning behind the differing positions.

It is safe to say that, given the extensive usage of Greek loanwords in rabbinic literature, some of the sages were familiar to a greater or lesser extent with ideas expressed by the Greeks and Romans in the areas of rhetoric, hermeneutics, and jurisprudence. There has been renewed interest and intense study of Roman legal theory and practice and their influence on the Mishnaic corpus.[19] New research by

Niehoff and Paz[20] into parallel phenomena and terminology in Homeric scholia and rabbinic literature has raised the possibility of their influence on midrashic techniques. A half decade after Tzvi Novick's 2014 essay on "Scripture as Rhetor," Richard Hidary has traced what he believes to be the profound effect of Greco-Roman rhetoric on Talmudic argumentation and midrashic composition alike.[21] Long ago, Menahem Luz has pointed to Jerusalem Talmud passages that are familiar with the figure of a Cynic philosopher.[22]

Yet all these interesting parallels and possibly even influences notwithstanding, it appears that philosophizing in the Greek mode was all but absent in rabbinic circles. The oral (and possibly written) creativity of the rabbis came down to us in a manner and form that were constructed to preclude the full integration of cultural phenomenon, such as philosophy and rhetoric, beyond sporadic appearances and influences. Were philosophic arguments excised by the later editors of rabbinic literature? I think not, given the fact that even the apodictic documents like the Mishna sometimes contain legal argumentation. This is not the case for philosophic argumentation. The rabbinic organization of learning around the Bible and around the Mishna, even if it was in imitation of the classical pedagogy around Homer as Bickerman claimed,[23] left little room for the introduction of systematic philosophic material. This fact is even more pronounced when we look at midrash. It is more than likely that some rabbinic figures were aware of Philo of Alexandria's early first-century attempt to compose a philosophic commentary on Scripture.[24] But it was the early Church fathers beginning with Clement of Alexandria and on to Origen of Alexandria and Caesarea who followed Philo's lead. It would seem that there were both linguistic (Greek language) and theological reasons (predilection for the allegorical) for the Christian adoption of the philosophic commentary pioneered by Philo and others. Rabbinic use of Hebrew in tannaitic times, in addition to Aramaic in amoraic times (albeit laced with some three thousand Greek and Latin loanwords),[25] led them away from philosophizing on Scripture, an activity that marked philosophic activity from Philo through Spinoza, according to Harry Wolfson.

But there was an inherent shared pedagogy between the Greek philosophic school and the Jewish sages of late antiquity. That was the pedagogy of questions and interrogation. In an enlightening essay, David Rosenthal showed how tannaitic sessions were structured around questions, often raised by the students.[26] But the topics and focus of these rabbinic question-and-answer sessions were wholly different from the philosophic academies or the schools of rhetoric. The rabbinic curriculum centered on legal discussion and biblical interpretation. Some of the hermeneutics and rhetoric surely were shared with or even borrowed from the larger ambient culture. But the subject matter for the rabbis was parochial and pointed inward—rabbinic legal discussion and transmission or inquiry (midrash) into the Bible. However, Greco-Roman culture and rabbinic culture both drew on the ancient wisdom schools of the Near East.[27] I continue to maintain that the oral culture promoted by the rabbis, encompassing legal debate and midrash and aggadic interpretation of Scripture, was designed to insulate the rabbinic movement and its adherents from the prevailing cultural winds of the Roman Empire.[28] So for example, the one rabbinic gesture to historical creativity is the tannaitic work Seder Olam that is also a far cry from historiography as represented in Josephus's Greek oeuvre.[29] Two hundred years of scholarly research has shown that the rabbinic effort to insulate and isolate from Greco-Roman influence was only partially successful. This was even more the case since some elements within the rabbinic movement, especially the political leaders such as Rabbi Judah the patriarch and the patriarchate in general, advocated a close relationship with Roman authorities and an openness to Greek culture.

The rabbis were not classical philosophers. The successful synthesis of rabbinic culture with Greco-Roman philosophy would have to wait for the gaonic period, and it was mediated through Arabic sources. Saadia Gaon, and later Maimonides and his followers, would integrate philosophy and rabbinic literature. The late antique rabbis did call themselves sages (*sophoi*), but they were not *philosophi*. Their love was for Torah, oral and written. This was their "wisdom," and their love was to search Torah in every aspect.

References

Abramson, Shraga (1953), "Mileshon ḥahamim," *Lěšonénu: A Journal for the Study of the Hebrew Language and Cognate Subjects* 19: 61–71.

Bickerman, Elias (1988), *The Jews in the Greek Age* (Cambridge, MA: Harvard University Press).

Brodsky, David (2014), "From Disagreement to Talmudic Discourse: Progymnasmata and the Evolution of a Rabbinic Genre," in Ronit Nikolsky and Tal Ilan (eds.), *Rabbinic Traditions between Palestine and Babylonia* (Leiden: Brill): 173–231.

Epictetus (1925), *Discourses, Books 1–2* (W. A. Oldfather, trans.), Loeb Classical Library 131 (Cambridge, MA: Harvard University Press).

Fischel, Henry A. (1973), *Rabbinic Literature and Greco-Roman Philosophy: A Study of Epicurea and Rhetorica in Early Midrashic Writings* (Leiden: Brill).

Furstenberg, Yair (2019), "Provincial Rabbis: Shaping Rabbinic Divorce Procedure in a Roman Legal Environment," *Jewish Quarterly Review* 109, no. 4: 471–499, https://www.jstor.org/stable/26900166.

Goldin, Judah (1965), "A Philosophical Session in a Tannaite Academy," *Traditio* 21: 1–21. http://www.jstor.org/stable/27830787.

Harvey, Warren Zev (1992), "Rabbinic Attitudes toward Philosophy," in Herman J. Blumberg (ed.), *Open Thou Mine Eyes: Essays on Aggadah and Judaica Presented to Rabbi William G. Braude on His Eightieth Birthday and Dedicated to His Memory* (Hoboken, NJ: Ktav): 83–101.

Hidary, Richard (2017), *Rabbis and Classical Rhetoric: Sophistic Education and Oratory in the Talmud and Midrash* (Cambridge: Cambridge University Press).

Hidary, Richard (2022), "The Greco-Roman West and Rabbinic Literature in Palestine and Babylonia," in Christine Hayes (ed.), *The Literature of the Sages: A Re-Visioning* (Leiden: Brill): 311–343.

Hirshman, Marc (1988), "The Greek Fathers and the Aggada on Ecclesiastes: Formats of Exegesis in Late Antiquity," *Hebrew Union College Annual* 59: 137–165.

Kister, Menahem (2013), "Allegorical Interpretations of Biblical Narratives in Rabbinic Literature, Philo, and Origen: Some Case Studies," in Gary A. Anderson, Ruth Clements, and David Satran (eds.), *New Approaches to the*

Study of Biblical Interpretation in Judaism of the Second Temple Period and in Early Christianity (Leiden: Brill): 133–183.

Kulp, Joshua (1997–2013), "English Explanation of Pirkei Avot," *Sefaria*, https://www.sefaria.org/English_Explanation_of_Pirkei_Avot?tab=contents.

Lieberman, Saul (1974), *Texts and Studies* (New York: Ktav).

Lieberman, Saul (1963), "How Much Greek in Jewish Palestine?" in *Biblical and Other Studies* (Cambridge, MA: Harvard University Press): 123–141, https://www.degruyter.com/document/doi/10.4159/harvard.9780674729582.c8/html.

Lieberman, Stephen J. (1987), "A Mesopotamian Background for the So-Called Aggadic 'Measures' of Biblical Hermeneutics?" *Hebrew Union College Annual* 58: 157–225, http://www.jstor.org/stable/23508256.

Luz, Menahem (1989), "A Description of the Greek Cynic in the Jerusalem Talmud," *Journal for the Study of Judaism* 20: 49–60.

Malka, Orit (2019), "Disqualified Witnesses between Tannaitic Halakha and Roman Law: The Archeology of a Legal Institution," *Law and History Review* 37: 903–936.

Malka, Orit, and Yakir Paz (2021), "A Rabbinic Postliminium: The Property of Captives in Tannaitic Halakhah in Light of Roman Law," in *Legal Engagement: The Reception of Roman Law and Tribunals by Jews and Other Inhabitants of the Empire* (Collection de l'École Française de Rome 579) (Roma: École française de Rome): 323–344. http://digital.casalini.it/9782728314645.

Neusner, Jacob (2002), "The Formation of Rabbinic Judaism: From the Mishna's Philosophy to the Talmud's Religion," *Communio Viatorum* 44: 19–43.

Niehoff, Maren R. (2012), "Commentary Culture in the Land of Israel from an Alexandrian Perspective," *Dead Sea Discoveries* 19: 442–463, https://brill.com/view/journals/dsd/19/3/article-p442_7.xml.

Novick, Tzvi (2012), "Scripture as Rhetor: A Study in Early Rabbinic Midrash," *Hebrew Union College Annual* 82–83: 37–59.

Paz, Yakir (2022), *From Scribes to Scholars: Rabbinic Biblical Exegesis in Light of the Homeric Commentaries* (Tübingen: Mohr Siebeck).

Rosenthal, David (2017), "On Methods of Instruction in the Talmudic Era," in J. Hacker (ed.), *Wise Hearted: The World of the Sages* (Hebrew) (Jerusalem: Joseph Hacker), 39–54.

Safrai, Ze'ev (2018), "Liber Antiquitatum Biblicarum: A Para-Rabbinic Jewish Source Close to the Yavne Period," in Joshua Schwartz and Peter J. Tomson (eds.), *Jews and Christians in the First and Second Centuries: The Interbellum 70–132 CE* (Leiden: Brill): 401–426.

Shoval-Dudai, Nurit (2019), *A Glossary of Greek and Latin Loanwords in Post-Biblical Jewish Literature* (Hebrew) (Jerusalem: Academy of the Hebrew Language).

Sperber, Daniel (1984), *A Dictionary of Greek and Latin Legal Terms in Rabbinic Literature* (Ramat-Gan: Bar-Ilan University Press).

Sperber, Daniel (2012), *Greek in Talmudic Palestine* (Ramat Gan: Bar-Ilan University).

Wilfand, Yael (2019), "Did Roman Treatment of Freedwomen Influence Rabbinic Halakhah on the Status of Female Converts in Marriage?" in Y. Monnikendam and Paul J. du Lessis, *Family Law(s) under the Roman Empire, Journal of Legal History*: 182–202.

Wilfand, Yael (2021), "A Proselyte Whose Sons Converted with Him: Roman Laws on New Citizens' Authority Over Their Children and Tannaitic Rulings on Converts to Judaism and Their Offspring," in Katell Berthelot et al. (eds.), *Legal Engagement: The Reception of Roman Law and Tribunals by Jews and Other Inhabitants of the Empire* (Roma: École française de Rome).

Wolfson, Harry Austryn (1942), "The Double Faith Theory in Clement, Saadia, Averroes and St. Thomas, and Its Origin in Aristotle and the Stoics," *Jewish Quarterly Review* 33: 213–264, https://www.jstor.org/stable/1451992.

6
Mysticism and Rabban Yoḥanan ben Zakkai

The intense study of Jewish mysticism in the twentieth century, spurred on by Scholem's monumental work, left its mark also on the study of rabbinic literature and thought. In this chapter we will engage a source relating to Rabban Yoḥanan ben Zakkai that sees him as founding a tradition of mystical speculation.

The Mishna, the foundational digest of the oral Law, mentions explicitly three types of restricted subject matter, two of which are identified as mystical speculation,[1] the act (*maaseh*) of creation, speculating on how the world was created and what preceded creation, and the act (*maaseh*) of the chariot, based on Ezekiel's vision of God's chariot (m. Ḥagigah 2:1). It deems these two topics be restricted to the most intimate forum and warns against those who, engaged in mystical speculation, do not respect the honor/glory (*kavod*)[2] of the Creator.[3]

The central texts on mysticism revolve around this m. Ḥagigah 2:1, beginning there, moving on to the Tosefta, t. Ḥagigah 2:1–7, and finally to the two Talmuds. We will concentrate on t. Ḥagigah 2:1–2:

> They/We do not teach[4] (*ein dorshim*) forbidden relations to three, but they/we do exegete to two; nor the act of creation to two, but we do teach to one; nor the act of the chariot to one unless he was wise (or: a sage), and understood[5] by his own will.
>
> A deed (*maaseh*)[6] of Rabban Yoḥanan ben Zakkai who was riding on his donkey and R. Elazar ben Arach was driving the

donkey behind him. He (R. Eleazar) said to him: "My Master (*Rabbi*), teach me (*shane*) one chapter of the acts of the chariot." He (Rabban Yoḥanan) said to him: "Have I not said to you from the beginning that they/we do not teach (*shonin*; variant reading *dorshin*) the chariot to one unless he is wise (or: a sage), understanding on his own?" He (R. Elazar) said to him: "From now, I will lecture (*artze*)[7] before you." He (Rabban Yoḥanan) said to him: "Speak!" R. Eleazar ben Arach began to expound on the act of the chariot. He (Rabban Yoḥanan) alighted from his donkey and wrapped himself in his *tallit*,[8] and the two of them sat on a rock under an olive tree, and he (R. Elazar) lectured before him. Rabban Yoḥanan stood up and kissed him on his head and said: "Blessed is God, Lord of Israel, who gave a son to Abraham our father who knows how to fathom and teach the glory (*kevod*) of our Father in Heaven!" There are those who teach well (*naeh*) but do not practice well; those who practice well but do not teach well. Elazar ben Arach teaches well and practices well. Your joy, Abraham our father, that Elazar ben Arach came forth from your loins, who knows to fathom and teach the glory of our Father in heaven!

R. Yose son of R. Juda says: "R. Joshua lectured before Rabban Yoḥanan ben Zakkai, R. Akiva lectured before R. Joshua, and Ḥananiah ben Ḥinai lectured before R. Akiva."

This section of the Tosefta is composed of three parts. The first is a running gloss to the Mishna Hagigah. The second is a story about Rabban Yoḥanan ben Zakkai and one of his favored pupils, R. Elazar ben Arach. The third brief section is cited in the name of R. Yose ben Juda, and it presents the chain of the mystical tradition, beginning with Rabban Yoḥanan whose student R. Joshua lectured before him, presumably, due to the context, on mystical matters. The Tosefta then contains traditions about two pupils of Rabban Yoḥanan who were well versed in esoteric Torah. After we look more closely at the first two parts of the Tosefta, we will consider whether preference is given to one or the other of Rabban Yoḥanan's students, R. Joshua or R. Elazar.

The terse glosses in the Tosefta on m. Hagigah 2:1 give precise explanations to the lapidary formulations of the Mishna. The Tosefta holds that illicit relations are taught and interpreted before two pupils, the act of creation before one pupil and the act of the chariot again before one pupil, only after that person has shown independent understanding.[9] The verb in the Mishna and Tosefta for teaching/exegeting is *dorshin*, which would seem to indicate the activity of teaching and interpreting Scripture, *midrash* on these subjects.[10] We will move on to the story and review this definition of interpreting Scripture in its light.

As opposed to the later renditions of this story in the two Talmuds,[11] our story has no overt signs of mystical trappings, such as the appearance of angels and of mystical fire that are prominent in the Talmudic renditions. We have a matter-of-fact report of an extemporaneous session on mysticism in what would appear to be the most unlikely of circumstances. The teacher is riding a donkey, and his student is on foot following behind, guiding or attending to the donkey.[12]

Yet Rabban Yoḥanan's response—getting off the donkey, sitting, and wrapping himself—clearly indicates an extraordinary solemnity and formality, paralleled only by a story in t. Pesahim 2:16, concerning the formal annulment of a vow.[13] These two occurrences contrast sharply with stories and reports of regular legal discourse that takes place among the sages in the markets and on the road.[14] However, the setting in our Tosefta allows for privacy, seated on a rock under an olive tree. Another verb, this time at the very heart of our source is *hirtza/hirtzeti*, which I rendered here "lecture," but literally may be translated as "recount," since the same verb is used for moneychangers counting money. In modern Hebrew, this verb has become the standard term for lecturing, and here it conveys the sense of the source. We do find, however, R. Akiva in t. Nidda 6:6 rejecting such a "report" and again using the word *hirzeti*. Indeed, the Tosefta is the richest of the tannaitic sources in its use of this verb, found only rarely elsewhere, and it is generally used when a scholar brings back a report to a fellow scholar of a conversation with another scholar, often abroad.[15]

Elazar ben Arach proves to his teacher that he is capable of expounding the mysteries of the chariot on his own, and receives both a kiss on the head and an effusive blessing from his teacher. We will take a closer look at the blessing. The formulaic opening is the same one that was in use, according to t. Ta'anit 1:11, for blessings in the temple, with its origin in Solomon's prayer (1Kgs 8:15). The blessing is over the fact that God gave "a son" to Abraham—referring to Elazar Ben Arach. This repeats itself in the closing lines—"Your joy, Abraham our father, that Elazar ben Arach, came forth from your loins." This closing is paralleled closely twice in tannaitic literature. First, R. Joshua praises R. Elazar ben Azaria with this formula (Mekilta Bo 16) and the second instance where R. Tarfon exults over R. Akiva (Sifre Numbers 75). Our source's use of the blessing of R. Elazar ben Arach as being "Abraham's son" was explained by traditional commentators as referencing Abraham's ability to recognize God by his own devices,[16] at least according to the midrashic tradition. So, too, R. Elazar ben Arach was able to understand the *chariot*—mystical speculation about God, evidently also by his own authority and powers. Though the phrase "gave a son to Abraham" needs further elucidation, it is clear that the motif father/son plays a central role in this blessing with Elazar being both a son to Abraham and a son who knows how to respect the glory of his Father in Heaven.

R. Elazar ben Arach is praised for "teaching well and practicing well." The only other place in the Tosefta where we find "teaches and practices" is at t. Yevamot 8:7 when R. Elazar ben Azariah castigates Ben Azzai who teaches/exegetes well but does not practice well, since the latter remained a bachelor and did not fulfill the commandment to be fruitful and multiply. Is this a stock phrase? Or does it mean here that he indeed fulfilled the caveat of the Mishna that one must understand first by oneself and only then study with another? For now that seems to be the best interpretation.[17]

R. Elazar ben Arach is celebrated in this Tosefta, as he is also in the Mishna Avot, which we saw earlier in this book (Chapter 5). Yet, immediately after this lean and lovely story, later embellished in the two Talmuds with pyrotechnic descriptions, the Tosefta brings a statement by R. Yose ben Juda that amounts to a different "chain of tradition" of chariot mysticism. In this tradition, R. Joshua is feted as having "lectured" before his teacher Rabban Yoḥanan ben Zakkai as later R. Akiva lectured before his teacher R. Joshua. How does this chain of tradition with R. Joshua being the link between Rabban Yoḥanan ben Zakkai and R. Akiva relate to the previous story about R. Elazar ben Arach? Do they complement one another? Or, as is the case in the Mishna Avot we studied in Chapter 5, is there a debate over Rabban Yoḥanan's favored student of mysticism?

This chain of tradition in the Tosefta is followed by two stories. The first is the famous *pardes*, orchard, where R. Akiva alone, of the four sages who entered, survives the mystical experience "in peace." The next story recounts R. Joshua's meeting ben Zoma on the road (*istarta*), with the latter engaged in speculating on the act of creation, while walking on the road. Both these stories serve as ominous warnings, pointing to the dangers of mystical inquiry, since both end in the death of important and learned sages. Ben Azzai dies in what appears to be chariot speculation in the *Pardes*, while Ben Zoma dies subsequent to his engagement in speculation on the act of creation.

These few pages of the Tosefta are the earliest and most important witness to mysticism in tannaitic times. They are an elaborated version of the parallel at m. Ḥagigah 1:8–2:2. That Mishna is a vigorous statement of the Mishna's self-perception concerning the oral traditions it contains. Some scholars raised the possibility that this section of the Mishna Hagigah was an "early" Mishna, from Second Temple times.[18] Be that as it may, it certainly serves as a focused introduction to the entire project of the Mishna. Beginning at m. Ḥagiga 1:8, this Mishnaic introduction first explores the different subjects of the oral law and their roots in Scripture, surprisingly declaring some of the most central rabbinic laws, such as the laws of Shabbat, to be as "mountains hanging by a hair," with little support in Scripture. The Mishna goes on to detail restricted subjects, including *maaseh merkabah* (act of chariot) and *maaseh bereishit* (act of creation). It is good to point out that scholarship of the past century attributes these Mishnaic restrictions to the school of R. Akiba while the school of R. Yishmael did allow for teaching and expounding at least *maaseh bereishit*.[19] Finally, this introduction to the Mishna goes on to relate the history of the first (and only!) difference of opinion in the entire oral law through most of the Second Temple era, regarding the laying of hands on the sacrifice on a holiday.

The Tosefta will explain that this extraordinary unanimity was due to the decisions handed down by the seventy-one-member Sanhedrin that resolved all controversies. This unanimity broke down, according to our Tosefta, due to the proliferation of students of the early first-century sages Shammai and Hillel, students it is claimed, who did not attend their masters sufficiently. Our Tosefta, then, is a historiography of both the oral tradition and its esoteric branch.

I agree with those scholars who see the esoteric tradition hinted to in the Tosefta as the tip of the iceberg. I hold that a rich esoteric tradition flourished in rabbinic circles throughout the Tannaitic period and beyond. In a superb article, Alon Goshen-Gottstein canvassed the differing scholarly opinions on rabbinic mysticism and argued, on the basis of a close reading of our Tosefta passage, that one must distinguish between expounding Scripture that relates to the chariot and creation as opposed to achieving visions of God. According to his reading, the passages we quoted above pertained to Scriptural exegesis, whereas the famous "Four who entered the *Pardes*"[20] is about mystic practice and visions. He supports this by pointing out correctly that our passages use the verb *drs*—to teach, interpret or exegete—whereas the following famous passages of the "expedition" in the *Pardes* speak of seeing and glimpsing. Yet I think the distinction between exegetical reading and interpreting of mystical passages of Scripture and achieving a mystical experience is too sharply drawn.[21] This is clear already in the continuation of the Tosefta where ben Zoma says "he was 'looking' at the deeds of creation and between the upper waters and lower waters there is only a handbreadth as it says 'and God's spirit hovered.'" Ben Zoma deduces *from Scripture* the architecture of Genesis and calls his activity "*zofe*" (or *mistakel* in the Erfurt manuscript)—"I was looking." The Jerusalem Talmud parallel has R. Elazar ben Arach's talking about the chariot that leads to him and Rabban Yoḥanan being encircled by a wall of fire.[22]

Exacting, extensive research has forged the consensus that the bulk of rabbinic learning was transmitted orally throughout most of the rabbinic period.[23] This orality would necessarily limit the number of students, as one could gain access only through sitting at the feet of a sage or his "tanna"[24]—the "repeater," the oral amanuensis as it were, who had committed the oral Torah to memory. These teachings were eventually committed to writing in the post-rabbinic period, on the basis of the oral tradition, possibly student notes, sages' correspondence, and other sporadic written sources. How likely is it that the esoteric teachings of this oral scholarly community would find their way into the "published" rabbinic compendia of the gaonic, post-Talmudic period, in the early Middle Ages?

There is also outside evidence for rabbinic mystical learning provided by the church father Origen, who made a special effort to consult rabbinic traditions.[25] Origen flourished in the first half of the third century CE at the same time as tannaitic midrashic collections (e.g., Mechilta, Sifra, Sifre) were achieving their final oral, and more rarely written, form.[26] In the introduction to his impressive commentary on the Song of Songs, he remarks on the

"Hebrews" mystical tradition in the following well-known and oft cited passage:

> For they say that with the Hebrews also care is taken to allow no one even to hold this book in his hands, who has not reached a full and ripe age. And there is another practice too that we have received from them—namely, that all the Scriptures should be delivered to boys by teachers and wise men, while at the same time the four they call *deuterosis*[27]—that is to say, the beginning of Genesis, in which the creation of the world is described; the first chapters of Ezekiel, which tell about the cherubim; the end of that same, which contains the building of the Temple; and this book of the Song of Songs—should be reserved for study till the last.[28]

This is surely an excellent contemporary eyewitness to both instruction in elementary education "to boys by teachers and wise men" and to advanced restricted teaching for those who reached "a full and ripe age." The inclusion of Song of Songs and the last chapters of Ezekiel demands a long discussion that will not serve us here. For our purposes it is clear that Genesis and Ezekiel are the sources of inquiry for our *maaseh bereshit* (act of creation) and *maaseh merkabah* (act of chariot).[29] Origen's use of *deuterosis*, the Greek equivalent of the Hebrew word *Mishna*, seems to reflect our story's employment of that verb when Elazar ben Arach asks his teacher to teach (*shane*) him a chapter of the chariot.

But what was the content of these inquiries into mystical sections of the Scripture? We do have ben Zoma's interpretation of Genesis 1:2, brought in the Tosefta Hagiga mentioned above.[30] The setting there is that ben Zoma had not greeted R. Joshua properly when the two passed each other in the road (*istarta*), since ben Zoma had been occupied in speculating on *maase bereishit*. Hearing ben Zoma's interpretation, R. Joshua remarks sharply to his students that "ben Zoma is already outside." To be clear about the import of R. Joshua's cryptic statement, the Tosefta adds that ben Zoma passed away soon after. Was R. Joshua's verdict due to the nature of ben Zoma's interpretation, or was it because he was speculating while on the road, or because he did not greet his teacher properly due to his engrossment in *maase bereishit*?

Mystical aspirations were rife in the third-century Roman Empire and in Palestine in particular. Porphyry, born in nearby Tyre in the third century, recounts in detail the effort made by his teacher, the great Neoplatonist philosopher Plotinus, to achieve mystical union:

> To Plotinus "the goal ever near was shown": for his end and goal was to be united to, to approach the God who is over all things. Four times while I was with him he attained that goal, in an unspeakable actuality and not in potency only.[31]

Plotinus was reported to be accompanied by a *daimon*—a heavenly spirit.[32] A baraita, a tannaitic source outside of the Mishna, quoted in the Talmud, that sometimes tweaks these earlier sources, at b. Berakhot 7a, recounts the vision the high priest Yishmael ben Elisha had of God when entering the holy of holies. There is a long and well-documented history of priestly involvement in visions of God illuminated by Ithamar Gruenwald's penetrating essay.[33] The high priest Simon the Righteous recounts that when he entered the holy of holies, "one old man dressed in white and covered in white" would accompany him into the holy of holies on Yom Kippur (t. Sotah 13:9); entrance was allowed only to the high priest himself.[34] For Origen, the great third-century church father who is said to have studied with Plotinus,[35] the allegorical reading of Scripture leads to a mystical experience. These are the expressions Origen uses as collected by one scholar that reflect mysticism through exegesis:

> The language of union (e.g. *Comm. Cant.* 1.91.4 ff.; *Hom. Gen.* 10.5; *Comm. Jo.* 19.4), of intoxication or "enthusiasm" (e.g.,

Comm. Jo. 1.30; *Princ.* 4.1.6; cf. *Comm. Cant.* 3.185.24 ff., 220.15 f.), of vision (e.g. *Hom Num.* 27.12.273. 20 ff.; *Sel. Ps.*, PG 12.1349c ff.) or "seeing face to face" (e.g. *Princ.* 1.1.2; Hom. Josh. 3.1), is also regularly used where the spiritual reading of Scripture or the understanding of the divine is concerned.[36]

At least from tannaitic sources and on, the connection of the entrance into the holy of holies to a mystical vision is well documented (t. Sotah 9). The high priest's entrance into the conduit for God's presence and voice on earth surely helped nurture the link between the priesthood and mystical speculations. In the temple, God's otherwise ineffable name was pronounced by the high priest on Yom Kippur. According to tradition, this name had great powers in and of itself.

As both R. Akiva and Origen compared the Song of Songs to the Holy of Holies, entrance into Scripture became the path for meeting the Holy One—the goal of every mystic. As we have seen, R. Akiva attributed to the Torah creative powers. Beyond being the bedrock of Jewish culture, Scriptural study at its highest level was also the springboard for mystical experiences. The path was strewn with dangers, but those who were able to navigate it safely, as did R. Akiva, were, in the language of the Song, brought into the chambers of the King.

References

Armstrong, A. H. (1989) *rev., Plotinus*, (Cambridge, MA: Harvard University Press).
Bar-Asher Siegel, Michal (2014), "On the Meaning of '*Kehararim Hateluyim Beseara*,'" (Hebrew) *Leshonenu* 76: 137–148.
Fraenkel, Jonah (1977), "Remarkable Phenomena in the Text-History of the Aggadic Stories," *Proceedings of the World Congress of Jewish Studies* 3: 45–69, https://www.jstor.org/stable/23524679.
Goldin, Judah (1965), "A Philosophical Session in a Tannaite Academy," *Traditio* 21: 1–21, https://about.jstor.org/terms.

Goshen-Gottstein, Alon (2000), *The Sinner and the Amnesiac: The Rabbinic Invention of Elisha ben Avuya and Eleazar ben Arach* (Stanford, CA: Stanford University Press).

Griffith, Mark (2006), "Horsepower and Donkeywork: Equids and the Ancient Greek Imagination," *Classical Philology* 101: 185–246.

Gruenwald, Ithamar (1987), "The Impact of Priestly Traditions on the Creation of Merkabah Mysticism and the Shiur Komah," *Jerusalem Studies in Jewish Thought* 6: 65–120.

Halbertal, Moshe (2008), *Concealment and Revelation: Esotericism in Jewish Thought and Its Philosophical Implications*, translated by Jackie Feldman (Princeton, NJ: Princeton University Press).

Halperin, David J. (1980), *The Merkabah in Rabbinic Literature* (New Haven, CT: American Oriental Society).

Kahana, Menahem (2006), "The Halakhic Midrashim," in Shmuel Safrai et al., eds., *The Literature of the Sages*, second part (Royal Van Gorcum: Fortress Press): 3–105.

Kalmin, Richard (1999), *The Sage in Jewish Society in Late Antiquity* (London and New York: Routledge).

de Lange, Nicholas (1976), *Origen and The Jews* (Cambridge: Cambridge University Press).

Lawson, R. P. (1957), *Origen: The Song of Songs Commentary and Homilies* (Westminster: The Newman Press).

Macleod, C. W. (1971), "Allegory and Mysticism in Origen and Gregory of Nyssa," *Journal of Theological Studies* 22: 362–379.

Mandel, Paul (2017), *The Origins of Midrash: From Teaching to Text* (Leiden: Brill).

Niehoff, Maren R. (2016), "Origen's Commentary on Genesis as a Key to Genesis Rabbah," in Sarit Kattan Gribetz et al. (eds.), *Genesis Rabbah in Text and Context* (Tübingen: Mohr Siebeck): 129–153.

Niehoff, Maren R. (2020), "Homer between Celsus, Origen and the Jews of Late Antique Palaestina," in Jonathan Price and Rahel Zelnick-Abramovitz (eds.), *Text and Intertext in Greek Epic and Drama: Essays in Honor of Margalit Finkelberg* (London: Routledge): 185–209.

Niehoff, Maren R. (2021), "Celsus's Jew in Third-Century Caesarea: Tracing Hellenistic Judaism in Origen's Contra Celsum," in Michal Bar-Asher Siegal and Jonathan Ben-Dov (eds.), *Social History of the Jews in Antiquity: Studies in Dialogue with Albert Baumgarten* (Tübingen: Mohr Siebeck): 233–250.

Niehoff, Maren R. (2022), "Tracing Hellenistic Judaism in Caesarea: A Jewish Scholar of the Psalms in Origen's Gloss," (Hebrew) *Zion* 87: 7–36.

Origen, Alfons Fürst, and Holger Strutwolf (2016), *Der Kommentar Zum Hohelied*, Vol. 9/1 (Berlin: De Gruyter).

Stroumsa, Guy G. (2005), *Hidden Wisdom: Esoteric Traditions and the Roots of Christian Mysticism* (Leiden: Brill).

Tropper, Amram (2013), *Simeon the Righteous in Rabbinic Literature: A Legend Reinvented* (Leiden: Brill).

Zussman, Yaakov (2005), "Torah She-Be-'al-Pe'—Peshuta Ke-Mashma'a," in Yaakov Zussman and David Rosental (eds.), *Mehqere Talmud*, Vol. 3 (Jerusalem: Magnes Press): 209–384.

7

The Language of Creation

An Enduring Power

The mystical thrust extended itself to speculations on the power of the very language of the Torah.[1] The verse in Psalms 33:9, "For He spoke and it was," most likely, along with Genesis itself, inspired the tannaitic epithet for God, "The One who spoke and the world was."[2] This epithet, in turn, inspired the opening words of the blessing over the daily Psalms recitation, "Blessed is He who spoke and the world was." But, what language was God speaking when God said, "'let there be light' and there was light" (Gen 1:3) and "'Let the water below the sky be gathered into one area, that the dry land may appear.' And it was so" (Gen 1:9)?[3]

In a wonderful essay,[4] Milka Rubin shows that in Jewish circles from at least the second century BCE, from the book of Jubilees onward, the "mainstream" opinion was that God spoke Hebrew at both creation and revelation. The Talmud records a dissenting opinion positing that, if not at creation itself, at the very least, Adam spoke Aramaic in the Garden of Eden.[5] Aramaic, of course, was the lingua franca of the entire region for a millennium or more. The Greek and Latin Church fathers echoed the dominant Jewish position, but there, too, we find some dissenting opinions. The Syriac church fathers, however, endorsed Syriac, a dialect of Eastern Aramaic documented only from the first century CE, as the primordial language of creation.[6] In a stunning comment about revelation in the amoraic midrash Pesiqta de Rab Kahana, R. Nehemia asserts that the first word of the Ten Commandments, *anokhi*, was in the Egyptian language,[7] an accommodation for the children of

Israel who had learned the language of their hosts. The illustrative parable that follows puts it more starkly: God spoke in the language of their captors. With these minor and rare exceptions, Hebrew the holy language was God's language.

The aggadic midrash, Genesis Rabbah, advances the following insight:

> R. Isi said: In four places, this locution was said, "Make yourself." Three of them were clarified, but the one not: "Make yourself an ark *of gopher wood*" (Gen 6:14) ... "Make yourself *flint* knives (Josh 5:2) ... "Make yourself two *silver* trumpets" (Num 10:2). "Make yourself a *saraph*"[8] (Num 21:8) was not clarified. R. Judan in the name of R. Isi, "The wise man, hearing them, will gain more wisdom" (Prov 1:5): This is Moses. He said, "if I make it from gold or silver, this language (i.e., *zahav, kesef*) does not "fall" (i.e. resonate) on this language (*"neḥashim seraphim"* Num 21:6), but I shall make it of copper (*neḥoshet*), for this language "falls" (resonates) on this language, 'a copper serpent' (*neḥash neḥoshet*, Num 21:9)." From here you learn that Torah was given in the Holy language.
>
> Rabbi Pinchas and Rabbi Ḥezekia in the name of Rabbi Simon said: Just as the Torah was given in the Holy language, so too the world was created in the Holy language. Have you ever heard [someone] say: *gynei gynaia, ita itita, anthropei anthropaia, gavra gavrita*?[9] But *ish isha* [you do hear]? Why so? Since this language "falls" on this language (Gen Rab 31:8).[10]

This passage has a parallel in the Jerusalem Talmud, but here in Genesis Rabbah the emphasis is on word play as an exegetical device. "Language falling on language" is a technical term that is broader and more innovative than "midrash of names" that appears in the Talmudic parallel. That parallel in the Jerusalem Talmud (Rosh Hashana 3:9 59a, p. 676) is attributed to R. Yasa, and I quote the second half where the traditions differ: "'Make yourself a *saraph*.' Said Moses, 'Isn't it essentially a serpent?' Therefore, 'Moses made a copper serpent." From here R. Meir would interpret names (*doreish sheimot*)." This pared-down parallel does not use a term for the word play employed by Moses. Instead, it has R. Meir deduce from Moses's example that one should "interpret names" ("*dorshin sheimot*").[11] The two cases are nouns to be sure, *ish/isha* and *neḥash/neḥoshet*. Word play allows Moses to deduce of what material to make the serpent. It also allows Adam to deduce the correct name for his female partner. In both cases, the word play exists only in Hebrew, which allows R. Isi and R. Ḥezekia, respectively, to conclude that both in Moses's time and Adam's the language employed was Hebrew.[12]

More was at stake here than national pride. Another source, which predates the discussion above and is attributed to R. Akiva in m. Avot 3:14, says the following:

> Beloved are Israel, who were called the children of God (*hamakom*)... Beloved are Israel, for they were given an (precious[13]) instrument.
> An abundant love is made known to them since they were given the tool through which the world was created.

That powerful instrument was the Torah, itself a composition of divine Hebrew. The concept here is that the words of Torah are a creative force for the one who knows how to use them.[14] Those who espoused the ideology that the Torah was given in Hebrew were most probably aware of R. Akiva's statement. The corollary is that the Hebrew words of the Torah have the potential to continue to create in the hands of the sages. This creative power of Torah is the subject of the opening parable in Genesis Rabbah 1:1:

> R. Hoshaya opened,[15] "I was with Him as a confidant (*amon*), a source of delight" (Prov 8:30), *amon* (means) *pedagogue, amon* (means) covered, *amon* (means) hidden...
> Alternatively, *amon* (means) artisan (*uman*). The Torah is saying, "I was the artisan's instrument of God."

In the way of the world, a king of flesh and blood who builds a palace does not do so from his own mind, but rather from the mind of an architect, and the architect does not build it from his own mind, but rather has parchments (i.e., parchment plans, blueprints) and codices[16] in order to know how to make rooms and doorways. So too God gazed into the Torah and created the world.

Similarly the Torah says, "*Be'* (*Be'* =through me) *reishit* God created" and *reishit* means Torah, as in "God made me the beginning (*reishit*) of His way" (Prov 8:22)

R. Hoshaya[17] echoes R. Akiva's statement at the outset, reading the artisan's tool into Wisdom's autobiographical oration in Proverbs 8. Wisdom is identified as Torah already by the late Second Temple author Ben Sira in the second century BCE and later by the late antique rabbis.[18] Wisdom depicts herself in that speech as existing before creation and being God's companion. It was with the Torah's assistance that the world was created, but how?

In this passage of Genesis Rabbah, the comparison to a human king is meant to supply the answer. God looked into the Torah to create the world, it would seem, much as the king's architect looked into codices and tablets to build the palace. This comparison has been studied carefully by generations of scholars, especially in relation to similar but different comparisons in Philo of the first century CE and later in Origen of the third century CE.[19]

Before considering parallels to other authors, it is worthwhile to pay attention to the great sixteenth-century commentator on Genesis Rabbah, Shmuel Yaffe Ashkenazi, who raised a number of inconsistencies within the *mashal*, the illustrative parable quoted above. I quote at length in my own translation:

> How does he move from "craftsman" to "craftsman's instrument"?
> ... How does he derive "craftsman's instrument" from the verse (simply *uman*—a craftsman)

... Moreover according to the comparison he brings, neither this (craftsman) nor that (craftsman's instrument) "fits" the Torah, but the Torah is like the parchments and codices as he says later on "God looked into the Torah and created."

More difficult is that he cites "from the way of the world" etc., which is not comparable—it makes sense that a flesh and blood king who is generally not a builder needs a craftsman other than himself, but God who is the creator of everything, how can one say that God needs a craftsman?[20]

This great master of aggada goes on in his commentary to resolve these difficulties. I wish, however, to focus on his last query and suggest that the midrash here uses this comparison, not as generally understood but rather to contrast God's behavior with that of the king of flesh and blood.

Let us preface our reading with a text critical point. It is not at all necessary to posit that the comparison is authored by the same sage who opined *amon* (=companion)/*uman* (=craftsman). This anonymous comment introduced as an alternate explanation might very well stand alone, whereas the comparison moves it further by speaking of the craftsman's instrument rather than just craftsman. Now, even if we attribute the play on words *amon/uman* to R. Hoshaya, which in and of itself is far from certain in my view,[21] this third-century rabbi might simply have joined R. Akiva's comment to the creative word play, that the Torah was God's instrument of creation. Scholars for over 130 years have placed this statement, attributing it to R. Hoshaya, in conversation with the church father Origen, his fellow Caesarean. Bacher[22] saw R. Hoshaya's parable as influenced by Philonic thinking possibly mediated by Origen. Yet had R. Hoshaya been in dialogue with Christian scholars, would he have compared the Torah to a pedagogue? This same comparison is attributed to Paul in Galatians 3:24: "Wherefore the law (*nomos*) was our guardian (*paidogogus*) to bring us unto Christ, that we might be justified by faith." It is possible, but not likely.

Let us now turn to the comparison itself of God the creator and a king of flesh and blood who wishes to build a palace. A closer scrutiny of the usage of the literary topos which introduces the comparison "*benohag shebaolam*" "in the way of the world" affords new insight into the import of the comparison.

In Genesis Rabbah, the phrase "in the way of the world" (possibly translated also "in the custom of the world"), when used in comparison to God's ways, comes to emphasize how different God's ways are from those of a human king.[23] To offer an example or two—God alone is to be praised for creation, accomplished by God alone, as opposed to a king of flesh and blood who has others who bear the burden with him (Gen Rab 1:7). Another example is that God alone can shape a creation or a form in water, whereas a king of flesh and blood can do so only on dry land. Most, if not all, of these comparisons are of anonymous origin and not attributed directly to a named sage.[24]

As to the comparison of God the Creator to a king of flesh and blood who employs an architect who consults his parchment plans, I suggest that it be understood as emphasizing how *different* God's creation was from that of a human king. God needed no artisan or architect. God consulted as it were God's own plans, looking into God's Torah (the letters?) and subsequently created the world. The logic of the comparison would seem to dictate that the Torah here is parallel to the parchment/blueprint and indeed is itself a parchment. But a slavish one-to-one comparison will not do here. God's creation was entirely different from that of human creation. Remembering that Torah is equivalent to Wisdom, looking onto Torah might be saying that God in wisdom created the world.[25] The phrase "look into the Torah" appears only one other time in Genesis Rabbah 37:4, referring to youth studying Torah.[26]

To summarize, from the mid-second century in R. Akiva's formulation through R. Hoshaya of the third century and onto the comparison in Genesis Rabbah, the Torah was seen as instrumental in creation. It was and, to some, remained a powerful instrument in its original Hebrew, which when "looked into" may, according to some, grant special powers to its master.

The most emphatic expression of the power of Scripture is found in the midrash on Psalms, whose provenance remains an unresolved conundrum:

> Another word: "A Psalm of David when he fled..." (Ps 3:1)
> This is what scripture says "... No person can set a value on it" (Job 28:13).
> R. Elazar said, the sections of the Torah were not given in order, for had they been given in order, anyone who read them would be able to revive the dead and do wonders. Therefore, the order of the Torah was concealed, but it is revealed before the Holy One blessed be He, as it is said, "And who, as I, shall call, and shall declare it, and set it in order for me..." (Isa 44:7).
> R. Yaakov in the name of R. Aha, why was the section of Gog and Magog (i.e., Ps 2) juxtaposed to the section of Absalom (i.e., Ps 3), to let you know that an evil son is worse for his father than the wars of Gog and Magog.
> R. Joshua ben Levi attempted to sit on this book (and arrange it).
> A small voice (*bat qol*) went out and said, "do not awaken the slumberer."
> R. Yishmael[27] wished to sit on this book before Rebbe. He said, "it is written: 'well founded for all eternity, made of truth and justice.'" (Ps 111:8)

This midrashic passage is as stunning as it is opaque. We will begin with the opening (*petihta*), which is transparent. The verse in Job speaks about Wisdom, which the rabbis treated as a synonym for Torah. Now the biblical word for "value" in the verse, *erech*, is a synonym in rabbinic Hebrew for order (*seder*). Thus, the six orders of Mishna are called six "*erchei*" Mishna in the fifth-century Midrash Pesikta d'Rav Kahana (1:6= Songs Rabbah 6, 4, 2). The verse in Job is interpreted, then, with great ease by the third-century R. Elazar ben Pedat as meaning that no one, except God, knows the real order of the Torah sections (*parshiot*). Isaiah is invoked to prove that God alone calls (or reads-*kara*), declares, and sets in order (again the root *erech*). All this is clear. But how did R. Elazar arrive at the notion that if one were to reveal the order of the sections of the Torah one would be able to do miracles? Are we to view this as an authentic amoraic passage or a late passage containing medieval mystical notions? We will return to this question after following the further development of the passage.

We learn from R. Yaakov in the name of R. Aḥa's subsequent comment that the word "section" used in the proem, *parasha* in Hebrew, denotes a unit of Scripture which is named according to its content and subject matter. Here Psalms 2 and 3 are not indicated by their numbered order but rather as they were known according to their subject matter. Psalm 3 is patently connected to Absalom according to its title, but Psalm 2 was called Gog and Magog, the ultimate war of the end of days, only by virtue of rabbinic exegesis. So too, the opening in the proem speaks of sections of Torah as we find elsewhere in rabbinic literature, such as the section (*parasha*) of Sotah, the section (*parasha*) of Nazir, and so on. R. Yaakov in the name of R. Aha offers a useful and insightful message derived from the juxtaposition of the great war of Gog and Magog (Ps 2) with the rebellion of David's son Absalom (Ps 3).

The next two anecdotes pick up the theme of understanding a book, similar to where we left off prior to R. Yaakov. The two rabbis attempt to "sit on the book," either the book of Psalms or the Torah. Both rabbis are rebuffed—the one by a small voice and the other by his master. But what could "sit on the book" possibly mean? If we look at the first of the two rebukes—"do not awaken the slumbering"—this appears to echo the original insight that if one were to know the Torah in order, one might revive the dead. We might then vocalize the word *leyashev*—"to restore or settle." The preposition remains difficult. The second rebuff seems to indicate that the words of Torah are "well founded for eternity." The Hebrew is "*semuchim la'ad*," which in our context should be taken to mean they are eternally juxtaposed. I suggest that the entire endeavor of exegeting juxtaposition is premised on the notion that the sections of Torah are indeed in order and there is no mystery to solve. The two rebuttals would be on opposite sides of the issue—is the Torah at present in its proper sequence or not? We do know elsewhere that there is a debate over whether one should read meaning into the ordering of the sections of the Torah and their juxtaposition.[28]

What is abundantly clear in this provocative passage is R. Elazar's mystical stance that by repositioning the sections of Torah into their real sequence one would have the power to revive the dead. Wilhelm Bacher remarked long ago that this is probably related to R. Akiva's view in Avot that Israel was given the instrument (i.e., the Torah) through which the world was created, repeated by R. Hoshaya at the beginning of Genesis Rabbah.[29] Abraham Joshua Heschel connects this statement with one of R. Elazar's teachers, Rav, who asserts that the biblical artisan Bezalel knew how to combine letters with which the world was created.[30] Gershom Scholem also noted this mystical passage.[31] What is interesting, then, is the notion that it is the sequence of sections that empowers the possessor of Torah, not the letters—as if one needs the right combination of sections to acquire the power of Torah.

The following two stories move back in time to a transitional figure between tannaim and amoraim, R. Joshua ben Levi, and finally to the late tanna, R. Yishmael ben R. Yosi. Both stories recount a thwarted attempt by a sage to discover the original order of the book (Torah, Psalms?), if I am correct in linking the stories to the opening homily. The verb to "arrange" in the first story echoes that opening homily about the order being hidden. The second story has Judah the Patriarch[32] invoking the "eternity" of the present order based on Psalms 111:8. That same verse is invoked in the

Babylonian Talmud's rendition where R. Abbahu rebuffs a heretic who allegedly refuses to interpret juxtaposition. I would, I suppose ironically, reverse the order of this midrashic section and play it in reverse, which would be its proper chronological order. R. Yishmael (the son of R. Yosi according to some manuscripts) was portrayed on more than one occasion as sitting before Rebbe, Judah the Patriarch. The patriarch here rebuffs R. Yishmael's attempt to bring order to the book, claiming that the present order is eternal. The relationship of this position to Rebbe's debate with R. Akiva at the beginning of Sifre Numbers 131 can be framed in different ways. There Rebbe objects to R. Akiva's rule that "every *parasha* that is adjacent to its friend, learns from it." Rebbe retorts, "Many *parashiyot* are adjacent but distant from another as east from west." Menahem Kahana, in his magisterial commentary to Sifre Numbers, contends that Rebbe is only taking exception to R. Akiva's claiming juxtaposition for all the *parashiyot*. Kahana goes on to cite a place where Rebbe employs juxtaposition, though, as he notes, the attribution is not unequivocal.[33] In our passage, Rebbe is insistent on preserving the present order of Scripture, and this does not imply necessarily his position on whether one should interpret juxtaposition.

In the following comment, again reading in reverse, R. Joshua ben Levi, a generation later and a mystical figure in rabbinic lore, attempts also to "rearrange" and is hushed by the *bat qol*, the small voice, that adjures him not to revive the dead. Had this story about Joshua ben Levi been known to R. Elazar, in the next comment in our section, it might very well have served as the trigger for R. Elazar's opinion that the knowledge of the right order of Scripture may empower one to revive the dead. This might be a more proximate lesson that engendered R. Elazar's thinking, rather than Bacher's correct reference to the precedent set by R. Akiva and others, that through Torah the world was created. Rabbinic literature contains some accounts of sages who were thought to have the power to revive the dead through their prayer. R. Ḥiyya and his children are represented in b. Bava Metzi'a 81a as being on the cusp of reviving the dead after bringing winds and rain with their prayer. Rava brings R. Zeira back to life by praying for his Purim drinking partner whom he had slaughtered (b. Meg. 7a). There are also traditions that knowledge of the forty-two-letter name of God gives power to its possessor—certainly to harm but possibly to heal.[34] Likewise there are legends about grass that can quicken the dead (Lev Rab 22:4). But what evidence, if any, do we have in late antiquity that a book of Scripture was intentionally "scrambled" in order to hide its power? There are none that I know of. My sense, and I am reaffirming Bacher's view, is that these passages in Midrash Tehillim are authentic and belong to amoraic literature and should not be deemed a part of later medieval mystical speculation. One might posit some connection between our passage and the power attributed to the laws (or book) of *Yezira*, creation, which two sages studied every Friday and by them successfully created livestock (b. Sanh. 65a). Above all, the passage in Midrash Psalms reflects the sages' belief in the power of Torah, a divine document that had, in their view, an unrealized potency. God's words in God's books necessarily were powerful and had a hidden power that was as yet unrealized

Is this a precursor of the very developed mystical systems of the late Pietists of Ashkenaz and other Kabbalistic works? Or is this simply another motivating device for plumbing the depths of the Torah and its structure? It would seem that the power of Torah was to be captured in its original language while unlocking the secret of its order. Did this Wisdom=Torah lend itself to translation? In the next chapter, we will continue to reflect on the power of Torah in the views of the rabbis and sages.

References

Bacher, W. (1891), "The Church Father, Origen, and Rabbi Hoshaya," *The Jewish Quarterly Review* 3, no. 2: 357–360, https://doi.org/10.2307/1449888.
Badalanova Geller, Florentina (2021), "Glottogenesis, the Primordial Language and the Confusion of Tongues," in Tatiana Slavova et al. (eds.),

Festschrift Anna-Maria Totomanov (Sofia: Universitetsko Izdatelstvo "Sv. Klime."): 324–363.
Braude, William G. (1975) *Pesikta De-Rab Kahana*, (Philadelphia: Jewish Publication Society).
Elitzur, Z. (2014), "Sinai between Oral and Written Revelation from Jubilees to the Amoraim," (Hebrew) *Zion* 79, no. 3: 291–325, https://www.jstor.org/stable/23982282.
Eshel, Esther, and Michael E. Stone (1993), "The Holy Language at the End of Days in Light of a New Fragment Found at Qumran," *Tarbiẓ* 62: 169–177, https://www.jstor.org/stable/23598743.
Fraade, Steven D. (2023), *Multiligualism and Translation in Ancient Judaism* (Cambridge: Cambridge University Press).
Fraenkel, Jonah (1991), *Darkhei ha-ggada vehamidrash*, 2 vols. (Givataim: Yad Letalmud).
Kogut, S. (1982), "לזאת יקרא אשה כי מאיש לקחה זאת" (Gen. 2:23)—A Folk Etymology?" (Hebrew) *Tarbiz* 51, no. 2: 293–298, https://www.jstor.org/stable/23595990.
Mandel, Paul (2018). "Between Tannaim and Amoraim: Changes in Hermeneutic Awareness during the Talmudic Period," (Hebrew) *Daat: A Journal of Jewish Philosophy & Kabbalah* 86: 117–136, https://www.jstor.org/stable/26895568.
Mandelbaum, Bernard (1962), *Pesikta de Rav Kahana* (New York: The Jewish Theological Seminary of America).
Marmorstein A. (1937/1968), *The Old Rabbinic Doctrine of God* (Oxford: Oxford University Press).
Moss, Yonatan (2010), "The Language of Paradise: Hebrew or Syriac? Linguistic Speculations and Linguistic Realities in Late Antiquity," in Markus Bockmuehl and Guy G. Stroumsa (eds.), *Paradise in Antiquity* (Cambridge: Cambridge University Press), 120–137, https://www.cambridge.org/core/product/identifier/CBO9780511760648A017/type/book_part.
Niehoff, Maren R. (2005), "Creatio Ex Nihilo Theology in Genesis Rabbah in Light of Christian Exegesis," *Harvard Theological Review* 99: 37–64.
Origen (1982), *Homilies on Genesis and Exodus*, Ronald E. Heine (trans.), The Fathers of the Church 71 (Washington, DC: Catholic University of America Press).
Origen, Marguerite Harl, and Nicholas De Lange (1983), *Origène, Philocalie, 1–20. Sur Les Écritures, et La Lettre à Africanus Sur L'histoire de Suzanne* (Paris: Les Editions du Cerf).
Philo (1929), *On the Creation*, F. H. Colson and G. H. Whitaker (trans.), Loeb Classical Library 226 (Cambridge, MA: Harvard University Press).
Rubin, M. (1998), "The Language of Creation or the Primordial Language: A Case of Cultural Polemics in Antiquity," *Journal of Jewish Studies* 49, no. 2: 306–333, https://doi.org/10.18647/2120/JJS-1998.

Urbach E. E. (1975), *The Sages: Their Concepts and Beliefs*, translated from Hebrew by Israel Abrams (London and Cambridge, MA: Harvard University Press).

Weiss, Tzahi (2018), *"Sefer Yeṣirah" and Its Contexts: Other Jewish Voices* (Philadelphia: University of Pennsylvania Press).

8

Torah Study

A Double-Edged Sword

Torah study was the preeminent value in the sages' religious worldview, though there were other minority approaches, as we saw in Chapter 3, where the Tosefta gave pride of place to charity and acts of lovingkindness. The elevation of Torah study above all else shaped the Jewish value system from Mishnaic times and continued to inform Jewish culture through our own times. This needs no further elaboration, having been the subject of numerous monographs and articles.[1] I wish to raise a different question, especially in light of our previous chapter on mystical speculation. Were there dangers attendant to Torah study? What was the goal of Torah study? Were there admission requirements to become a student of the sages (*talmid ḥachamim*)?[2] We will begin with a sugya, a sustained Talmudic section that will position us to answer the first of these questions and reflect on the others.

In the context of a discussion of the Temple ark at b. Yoma 72b, R. Yoḥanan reflects on the three pieces of the Temple furniture that were gilded with a gold molding (*zer*):

> R. Yoḥanan said: There were three (golden) moldings (*zer*): of the altar, of the ark and of the table. Of the altar: Aaron merited it; of the table: David merited it; of the ark, it is resting (in place), anyone who wishes to take (it), come and take (it). Lest you will say it is inferior to them all, the verse states "Through me kings will reign" (Prov 8:15).

Rabbi Yoḥanan queried: It is written *zr* (Exod 25:11), and we read *zer*, (If) one merits it is a wreath [*zer*]³ for him; (but if) one does not merit it,⁴ it is a stranger [*zara*] to him.

Rabbi Yoḥanan queried: It is written: "And you shall make for yourself a wooden ark" (Deut 10:1) and it is written: "And they shall make an ark of acacia wood" (Exod 25:10); From here (we learn), to a student of the Sages (*talmid ḥacham*) that the people of his town are commanded to perform his work for him.

"Overlay it, inside and out" (Exod 25:11). Said Rava: any student of the Sages whose inside is not like his outside, is not a student of the Sages.

Said Abaye, or say Rabba bar Ulla, he is called loathsome, as it is stated: "What then of one loathsome and foul, man who drinks iniquity like water" (Job 15:16).

Said Rabbi Shmuel bar Naḥmani: said Rabbi Yonatan: What is that which is written: "What good is money in the hand of a fool to buy wisdom, when he has no heart?" (Prov 17:16)? "Oy" to them to the enemies of the students of the Sages,⁵ who occupy themselves in Torah but have no fear of Heaven.

Proclaimed Rabbi Yannai: A pity on him who has no courtyard but makes a gate for his courtyard.

Said Rava to the Sages: I beg of you, do not inherit hell (*geihinom*) twice.

Said Rabbi Joshua ben Levi: What is that which is written: "And this is the Torah which Moses set [*sam*] before . . . (Deut 4:44)? If one merits—it becomes for him a drug [*sam*] of life; if one does not merit, it becomes for him a drug of death. And this is what Rava said: For one who is dexterous⁶ in it, a drug of life; for one who is not dexterous in it, it is a drug of death.

Said Rabbi Shmuel bar Naḥmani: Rabbi Yonatan queried: It is written: "The precepts of the Lord are right, rejoicing the heart" (Ps 19:9), but it is written: "The word of the Lord is pure" (Ps 18:31)? For one who merits, it gladdens him; for one who does not merit, it refines him. Reish Lakish said: This emerges from the verse itself: For one who merits, it refines him to life; for one who does not merit, it refines him to death.

"Fear of the Lord is pure, it stands forever" (Ps 19:10). Said Rabbi Ḥanina: This is one who studies Torah in purity. What is that? One who marries a wife and afterward studies Torah.

"The testimony of God is faithful" (Ps 19:8). Said Rabbi Ḥiyya bar Abba: She (Torah) is faithful to testify about those who study her.

In this extended composition, Land of Israel amoraim make the following claims:

1. Torah is available to all (R. Yoḥanan: "come and take").
2. Torah can have a positive or negative effect. It depends on the merits of the student (R. Yoḥanan: "wreath or stranger"; R. Joshua ben Levi: "drug of life or death"; R. Yonatan: "gladdening or refining"; Reish Lakish: "refine for life or for death").
3. The townspeople are instructed to pitch in to do the work of the student of the sages on the student's behalf.[7]
4. Fear of Heaven is both the goal and necessary prerequisite for the Torah student (R. Yonatan: Torah without Fear of Heaven is worthless; R. Yannai: Torah is the gateway to the courtyard which is Fear of Heaven).

The framework of this mini-sugya on Torah learning is a succession of remarks attributed to Land of Israel amoraim, which has been spliced into the larger sugya treating the clothes of the high priest and later the Temple furniture. Within this Land of Israel mini-sugya, the mid-fourth-century Babylonian sage Rava's voice is interwoven three times. He stakes out the following positions:

1. A follow-up comment to R. Yoḥanan's view on the community's responsibility to a student of the Sages, Rava

raises a proviso—A student of the sages whose "inside" is not the same as "outside" (inner thoughts and outward actions?) is not considered a student of the sages.
2. An enigmatic statement that follows on the importance of the fear of Heaven bidding students not to inherit hell twice-over.
3. An aramaic version of the preceding Land of Israel view of Torah as a drug of life or death nuanced as one who is dexterous in Torah or not.

The entire section is structured first around four comments that are homiletic readings of Exodus 25:10–11, which interpret the verses about the ark as indicating the availability of Torah, its double-edged nature depending on one's merits and finally the responsibility of the community to worthy students of Torah. The last three comments in the section are homilies on Psalms 19:8–10, verses that indeed treat the nature of Torah. These are interpreted as treating again the two-sided nature of Torah: life-giving and joyous, or painful and poisonous, depending on the "merits" and dexterity of the student.

We will focus on the formula that appears four times in this brief sugya: "if one merits it ... but if not ..." This formula makes its first appearance in t. Eduyot 1:14 in a fascinating debate between R. Akiva and the sages around the verse "I will fulfill the number of your days." R. Akiva holds that if one merits it, one completes the days allotted to that individual; if not, one's days are decreased. The sages hold that merit can bring additional days to those allotted, whereas lack of merit can bring a decrease. Another Tosefta source, Sotah 5:9, expands the formula to "if one merits *to Heaven* ... if not ..." Aside from our sugya above, the expression appears another five times in the Babylonian Talmud, once in the Jerusalem Talmud and more than seven times in Genesis Rabbah.[8]

This brief tally of the formula, and its relative rarity, serves to highlight the extraordinary and pivotal role it plays in our sugya.

Its role here is to emphasize that acquiring Torah knowledge can be potentially dangerous unless one is meritorious. What is that merit? I suggest that the answers are literally central to the sugya. Rava speaks of integrity—one whose inside is the same as outside. R. Yonatan and R. Yannai see Torah study as worthless without fear of Heaven. Finally, the end of the sugya, this passage, emphasizes purity in study, which is available only to the student of Torah who is married.

A similar note is struck at b. Shabbat 31a, with some overlap between these sugyot. In a famous passage where R. Simon ben Lakish counts out the six orders of Mishna, tallying each one with a word in the verse at Isaiah 33:6—*emunah*, seeds; *itecha*, seasons; *ḥosen*, women; *yeshuot*, damages; *ḥochmat*, holy things; *vadaat*, purities. His homily ends with the final words of the verse, "even so 'the fear (*yirat*) of God is his treasure.'" This is, as in our sugya, followed by the Babylonian Rava glossing the same verse in Isaiah in a different way but ending like R. Simon ben Lakish with the ultimate test being one's fear of God.

> Rava said: when a person is brought to judgment they say to him: Did you conduct business faithfully (*be-emunah*)? Did you designate times (*itim*) for Torah? Did you engage in procreation (*ḥosen*)? Did you look forward to salvation (*yeshua*)? Did you turn over and over again[9] in wisdom (*ḥochmat*)? Did you understand (*vadaat*) one thing from another? And, even so, if there is fear (*yirat*) of the Lord, yes, if not, no.

After a parable that posits fear of God as the sustaining element that preserves Torah, two other statements return to fear of God as the entrance requirement to study Torah:

> Rabba bar Rav Huna said: Any person who has Torah in him but does not have fear of Heaven is like a treasurer [*gizbar*] to whom they gave the inner keys but the outer keys they did not give him.

With what will he enter? Proclaimed Rabbi Yannai: A pity on him who has no courtyard but makes a gate for his courtyard.

As I record these statements, I am struck, on the one hand, by the prominence given fear of Heaven here, as opposed to its relative paucity elsewhere. Indeed, the end of the sugya in Shabbat is a paean to the fear of Heaven. It continues:

> R. Judah said: The Holy One, Blessed be He, only created His world so that people would fear before Him, as it is stated: "And God has so made it that men should fear before Him" (Eccl 3:14).
> R. Simon and R. Elazar were sitting. R. Ya'akov bar Aḥa was passing by. One said to his friend: "Let us stand before him as he is a man who fears sins."[10] The other said to him: "Let us stand before him, as he is a man of Torah." He said to him: "I said to you that he is a man who fears sins, and you said to me he is a man of Torah?"
> Conclude that it was R. Elazar who said: "because he is a man who fears sin," since R. Yoḥanan said in the name of R. Elazar: The Holy One, Blessed be He, has in His world only fear of Heaven alone, as it is stated: "And now, Israel, what does the Lord your God ask of you, but to fear the Lord your God" (Deut 10:12). And it is written: "And unto man He said: Behold [*hen*], the fear of the Lord, that is wisdom" (Job 28:28).

But what is fear of Heaven? George Foot Moore suggests that Simon the Righteous's statement at m. Avot 1:3: "the fear of Heaven should be upon you," should be understood in modern terms as "reverence for God."[11]

These two extended passages in the Babylonian Talmud promote a view that resolves the dilemma of Torah study being potentially deleterious. The notion that Torah is potentially positive or negative goes back to the tanna R. Benaya at Sifre Deuteronomy 306 that will be discussed below.[12] His answer is that Torah must be studied "for its own sake," evidently meaning with no intention of gaining prestige or material benefits. The later amoraic passages we've engaged here suggest a different approach. Reverence for God is the prerequisite for proper Torah study. Only this reverence can prevent one from the potentially negative power of Torah.

Interestingly, we find the pairing of these two concepts in a prayer attributed to Rav, the founding sage of the Babylonian academy Sura. He recited this short prayer immediately after completing the Amidah, the centerpiece of daily prayer.[13] His prayer is a supplication for a rich and fulfilling life, repeating the word *life* (*ḥayim*) itself eleven times. The penultimate supplication is for "a life that has love of Torah and fear of heaven" (b. Berakhot 16b). Rav has taken the binary opposition of love and fear and assigned the one to Torah and the other to God. This theological innovation is at the heart of the two passages of the Talmud we've studied here.

The dominant theme in rabbinic Judaism is the privileging of Torah study over all else. Not only that, but some sages proposed that Torah study had the power to both protect and heal. These themes are developed at b. Sotah 21a (protection) and b. Eruvin 54a (healing). The notion that Torah can alleviate pain and illness was developed by the early third-century Land of Israel amora R. Joshua ben Levi, taking his cue from the paean to Wisdom at Proverbs 3–4: "They (words of Wisdom) are life to those who find them, healing for one's whole body" (Prov 4:22). The fourth-century Babylonian sage R. Joseph held that Torah protects and saves one who studies it. This position is challenged and is revised by his student Rava. Rava asserts that Torah is salvific only while one is actively engaged in its study. According to Rava, previous periods of study, however, can give a measure of protection, though not salvation, even when one is not engaged currently in study.

If there was a long and respected tradition that Wisdom and Torah bring benefit and blessing to their possessor, when and why did this new idea of the possible dangers of Torah arise?

It is the early third-century R. Benaya at Sifre Deuteronomy 306 who first expresses the perilous aspect of Torah for one who studies it improperly. In the Sifre he addresses the student of Torah directly in second person:

> If you do words of Torah for their own sake (*lishmam*) it is life for you as it says, "they are life to one who finds them" (Prov 4:22). But, if you don't do words of Torah for their own sake, they put you to death, as it says, "let my teaching come down (*yaarof*) as rain" (Deut 32:2). And "come down" (*arifa*) is nothing other than language of killing, as it says, "There in the *wadi* they shall break (*arfu*) the heifer's neck" (Deut 21:4).

R. Benaya's adjuration is in line with other exhortations in the Sifre that ask that one should not learn in order to receive the title of Sage or Rabbi, or some other advantage. R. Benaya is certainly more vehement. This definitely conflicts with a contemporary of R. Benaya, the great Babylonian sage Rav, who advocated study even when not undertaken "for its own sake," arguing that the power of Torah was such that it will become study for its own sake.[14]

If there is evidence for the presence of this new concept—"study for its own sake," *Torah lishma*—in tannaitic literature, I have not yet found it, aside from R. Benaya's statement at the close of the period. The legal term *lishma* alone without describing Torah appears in various contexts in tannaitic literature, ranging from bills of divorce that need to be written specifically for the person intended, to sacrifices that need to be intended for the specific sacrifice offered. Why would this early third-century Land of Israel sage, R. Benaya, transfer this legal concept to Torah study and go as far as to threaten death to one who studies for other reasons?

Who were the foes against whom R. Benaya hurled his threat? Büchler contextualizes this statement within the friction between the sages and parts of the general Jewish populace in Sepphoris.[15] R. Benaya, according to this, was trying to discourage inappropriate study that would not produce the character necessary to be a sage and thus add fuel to the animosity toward sages. Büchler goes on to play with the notion that the attraction to achieve the status of a sage, which included tax dispensations, wealth, or a place in the World to Come (as raised at Sifre Deuteronomy 41), brought students who were not really studying Torah for its own sake.[16] I am doubtful, though, whether this was sufficient reason to issue a veritable death threat to those prospective students. It seems too harsh, especially in light of the statement of R. Benaya's older contemporary, R. Eliezer ben R. Yosi Hagalili, who interpreted those same words of Deuteronomy as meaning that "words of Torah atone for all sins,"[17] including bloodshed!

I speculate that R. Benaya here is countering Jews and non-Jews who studied Torah as prophesying the coming of Jesus and the Christian movement. The specter of Christianity and its interpretation of Scripture often triggered this type of severe response from the sages from the second century on. Thus, R. Yishmael[18] is quoted at t. Shabbat 13:5 as saying that the books of *minim* create enmity between God and Israel and goes on to bolster his view with the verse "won't I hate those who hate God" (Ps 139: 21–22). One has no obligation to try to save the lives of those *minim*, who are quite clearly to be identified here as Christians.[19]

It is Sepphoris, where R. Benaya's study hall was located in the third century, which serves as the location of the first recorded Jewish-Christian conversation in rabbinic literature. t. Hullin 2:2 reports a second-century encounter between R. Eliezer ben Hyrcanus and Ya'akov of Kefar Sikhnin, where R. Eliezer relishes Ya'akov's "heretical" words in the name of Jesus ben Pantera. Sepphoris was a little over an hour's walk from Nazareth. Sepphoris had been granted the status of regional capital of the lower Galilee, ever since Roman rule came to Palestine. The late second century saw Sepphoris regaining its stature as a well-appointed and developed city, possibly of as many as 20,000 inhabitants. R. Judah the patriarch chose it as the seat of his rule for seventeen years. Inscriptions there and in nearby Beit Shearim show a multilingual environment. Leah Roth-Gerson described Sepphoris's "double character, a Jewish city with a Greek tinge."[20] In such an environment one can imagine the Christian movement beginning to make inroads, and R. Benaya might have felt the urgency to "outlaw" nonrabbinic reading of Scripture. Yet Sepphoris will only see real Christian expansion in the fourth century. Our conjecture here is no more than that without having stronger evidence for a Christian presence in Sepphoris of the late second century.

I wish to note, in the wake of hearing a wonderful lecture by Menahem Kister entitled the "The Dark Side of the Torah,"[21] that the motif of the Torah having the capacity to kill in these rabbinic statements is I think wholly different from the Pauline doctrine that the law is the cause of sin and death. I have always seen these rabbinic statements in terms of the power of Torah. Like anything powerful, be it atomic energy or rhetorical acumen, the power can be used for good purposes, or no less it can be abused for bad. For the rabbis to say that if one does not merit it one may lose one's life by Torah, there is an acknowledgment that one needs to use its power in the correct fashion.

Yet the Talmudic passage at the beginning of our chapter is of a different order from R. Benaya's statement. In the Talmudic passage, study alone, even for its own sake, does not insure success. Only if one "merits" it, Torah will be beneficial. If not, Torah's effects might be deleterious. It would seem that the Talmudic sugya has veered from the redemptive and ameliorative effects of Torah and has set a new priority and possible prerequisite for Torah study, reverence for God.

It appears that one of R. Benaya's contemporaries, R. Joshua Ben Levi, whose view is cited in our Babylonian sugya, emphasized one's merit, rather than R Benaya's insistence on the proper motivation. The two stances are not necessarily in contradiction and might be pointing to the same idea: motivation is merit. Yet without seeing R. Joshua's statement in its original Land of Israel text, it remains a distinct possibility that the leitmotif of the Babylonian sugya—the language of merit—lies behind R. Joshua's formulation.

It is abundantly clear that b. Yoma 72a, along with the parallels we've cited, is insisting on a different approach to Torah learning that sees reverence, fear of Heaven, as a prerequisite for one who hopes to reap the benefits of Torah study. The time-honored view that attributed to Wisdom and Torah life-enhancing powers has been modified to privilege reverence over all else and to see it as the key to reaping the rewards of Torah study.

References

Bacher, W. Z. (1899), "Le mot 'Minim,' dans le Talmud, désigne-t-il quelquefois des chrétiens?" *Revue des Etudes Juives* 38: 38–46.

Bar-On, Shrage (2017), "The Art of the Chain Novel in b. Yoma 35b: Reconsidering the Social Values of the Babylonian Yeshivot," *Hebrew Union College Annual* 88 (2017): 55–58.

Büchler, Adolph (1909?), *The Political and the Social Leaders of the Jewish Community of Sepphoris in the Second and Third Centuries* (Oxford: Oxford University Press).

Büchler, Adolph (1967), *Studies in the Period of the Mishna and Talmud* (Hebrew) (Jerusalem: Mossad Harav Kook).

Hirshman, Marc (2009), *The Stabilization of Rabbinic Culture* (New York and Oxford: Oxford University Press).

Hirshman, Menachem (1994), "Clarifying the Concept Fear of Sin," (Hebrew) in S. Rosenberg, M. Idel and D. Dimant (eds.), *Mincha LeSarah* (Jerusalem: Magnes Press): 157–162.

Kahana, Menahem Izhak (2011), *Sifre on Numbers: An Annotated Edition* (Hebrew) (Jerusalem: Magnes Press).

Kister, Menahem (2007), "Romans 5:12-21 against the Background of Torah-Theology and Hebrew Usage," *Harvard Theological Review* 100, no. 4 (2007): 391–424.

Krumbein, Elyakim (2010), "Torah Lishmah: A Reappraisal" (Hebrew) *Hagut* 9: 39–63, https://www.jstor.org/stable/24008570.

Lieberman, Saul (1961), *Tosefta Ki-Fshutah* (New York: JTS Press).

Marmorstein, Arthur (1920/1968), *The Doctrine of Merits in Old Rabbinical Literature* (New York: Ktav Publishing House).

Moore, George Foot (1927/1962), *Judaism in the First Centuries of the Christian Era: The Age of the Tannaim* (Cambridge, MA: Harvard University Press).

Roth-Gerson, Leah (1987), *The Greek Synagogue Inscriptions in the Land of Israel* (Hebrew) (Jerusalem: Yad Ben Zvi).

Safrai, Shmuel, Menahem Stern, David Flusser, and W.C. van Unnik (1976), *The Jewish People in the First Century: Historical Geography, Political History, Social, Cultural and Religious Life and Institutions*, Vol. 2 (Assen: Van Gorcum).

de Villier, Pieter (2020), 'In Awe of the Mighty Deeds of God': The Fear of God in Early Christianity from the Perspective of Biblical Spirituality," in Ann W. Astell (ed.), *Saving Fear in Christian Spirituality* (Notre Dame: University of Notre Dame Press): 21–53.

9
Why Does Tannaitic Universalism Leave No Trace in Amoraic Literature?

A recent monograph on universalism in the work of Porphyry, the third-century Tyre-born philosopher, asserts that there was "a growing propensity toward universalism during the third century crises of the Roman Empire."[1] If we are to trust rabbinic attributions, it would seem that in rabbinic Judaism the trajectory was quite the opposite. Tannaitic Judaism in the second century shows a clear universalist thrust, though by no means a view shared by all of the sages. In amoraic literature, the universalist voice is silenced altogether. We will begin by outlining briefly the tannaitic views we have studied elsewhere,[2] and we will proceed deliberately to the enigma of the disappearance of universalism in amoraic views.

The Mishna (Rosh Hashana1:2) sees the first day of Tishrei as a day of judgment, in which all humanity, all who have come into the world, pass before God in review as a Roman legion ("*numeron*" in the Mishna) passes before its commander. R. Eliezer ben Hyrcanus was of the opinion that the world was created in Elul and the first human, Adam, was created on 1 Tishrei (Leviticus Rabbah 29:1). This day was the beginning of humanity. The God who created Adam and Eve and judged them for their sin that same day (according to the sages) now judges all of Eve and Adam's descendants on this day, Gentile and Jew alike.

The universalism of the early rabbinic sages was preceded by a long history of universalism from late biblical times, especially as an integral element of the End of Days, when God is to be acclaimed as sovereign of the entire world by all peoples. Seminal essays by Moshe Weinfeld and Jon Levenson[3] have shown the ideological battle in early Second Temple times between Jewish universalism, as in Second Isaiah, and particularism as evidenced in the book of Ezra. We have seen in the last decades, an attempt by scholarship, to uncover a similar ideological rift in the tannaitic academies, with some scholars attributing universalism, to a minor or major degree, to the school of R. Yishmael, and particularism to the school of R. Akiva.[4] This tannaitic debate revolved around the question of whether the Torah, when it was revealed at Sinai, was intended for all peoples rather than just for the Israelites. The debate took various forms. For example, Sifre Deuteronomy 345 claims the Torah was to be seen as the betrothed of Israel and therefore prohibited to any but Israel. R. Akiva, in another metaphor we saw in the previous chapter, sees the Torah as the instrument of creation which God handed over to Israel, God's children, much like a unique bequest to the people whom R. Akiva, in the wake of Deuteronomy 14:1, calls "children of God (*hamakom*) (m. Avot 3:14).

It is R. Yoḥanan ben Napḥa, the leading amora of the land of Israel in the third century CE, who, pursuing R. Akiva's sentiments, holds that a Gentile who studies Torah is liable to death (b. Sanhedrin 59a). The prohibition was not limited to Torah study but spilled over into other commandments, such as Sabbath observance. Resting on the Sabbath was the exclusive privilege of the Jewish people, and the Gentile was prohibited from such Sabbath observance.[5]

In this chapter, I will focus on a source which highlights the amoraic turn to an aggressive particularism. We have already seen that the amoraim continue and intensify the stance that the Torah was for Israel alone in their own times, but we will examine the extent of this particularism and search for any vestiges of universalism in amoraic thought. We read in Leviticus Rabbah, chapter 13:

> R. Simon ben Yoḥai began his discourse with the verse "He stood, and measured the earth" (Hab 3:6). That is, the Holy One took the measure of all peoples and found no people other than Israel worthy of receiving the Torah. The Holy One took the measure of all generations and found no generation other than the generation of the wilderness worthy of receiving the Torah. The Holy One took the measure of all mountains and found no mountain other than Sinai worthy of having the Torah given on it. The Holy One took the measure of all cities and found no city other than Jerusalem worthy of having the Temple built within it. The Holy One took the measure of all lands and found no land other than the Land of Israel worthy of being given to Israel.
>
> That is what is written, "He stood, and measured the earth, He beheld and drove asunder (*hitir*) the nations" (Hab 3:6).
>
> Rav said, "He freed their blood (*hitir*), He freed their money. He freed their blood, as it says, 'you shall not let a soul remain alive' (Deut 20:16); He freed their money as it says, 'you should eat the spoils of your enemies'" (Deut 20:14).
>
> R. Yoḥanan said, "He jumped them into Hell, as it was said, 'to leap (*nater*) with them upon the earth'" (Lev 11:21).
>
> R. Huna Rabba of Sepphoris said, "He freed (*hitir*) their belts, that is what is written, 'He undoes the belts of kings, and fastens loincloths on them'" (Job 12:18).
>
> Ulla of Bira in the name of R. Simon ben Yoḥai, (a parable to what is this similar) "to one who went to the threshing floor, and his dog and donkey with him. He loaded five *se'ah* on the donkey but on the dog, two. That dog was panting. He removed one and it was panting. Both, and it was panting. He said, 'loaded and unloaded you pant'. Likewise, even the seven commandments

that the children of Noah received, since they were unable to uphold them they stood and unloaded them on Israel."

Said R. Tanḥum bar Ḥanilai (a parable to what is this similar), "to a doctor who entered to visit two sick persons. One had enough in him to live and one did not have enough in him to live. The one who had enough in him to live, he said to him 'this and that do not eat'. The one who did not have enough in him to live, he said to him 'whatever he desires, give him'. Likewise, the nations of the world who are not to live in the World to Come, 'as with the green grass I give you all these to eat' (Gen 9:3). But to Israel who are to live in the World to Come 'these are the living things you may eat among all the beasts on earth'" (Lev 11:2).

This passage consists of four comments on Habakkuk 3:6, followed by two parables (*meshalim*). Both the opening statement and the first of the parables appear separately in the earlier tannaitic midrash Sifre Deuteronomy (311, 343):

Another thing: "When the Most High caused nations to inherit": When God gave Torah to Israel, He stood, looked and gazed, as its says, "He arose and measured the land. He saw and released the nations" (Hab 3:6). And there was no nation among the nations which was worthy of accepting the Torah but Israel, "He set the bounds of the peoples" (Deut 32:8) ...

Another thing: "And he said: God came from Sinai" (Deut 33:2): When God was revealed to give Torah to Israel, it is not to Israel alone that He was revealed, but to all of the nations. First, He went to the children of Esau, and He said to them: Will you accept the Torah? They said: What is written in it? He said: "You shall not kill" (Exod 20:12). They said: The entire essence of those people and their father (i.e., Esau) is a murderer, as it says "And the hands are the hands of Esau" (Gen 27:22), "And by your sword shall you live" (Gen 27:40).

He then went to the children of Amon and Moav and said to them: Will you accept the Torah? They said: What is written in it? He said, "You shall not commit adultery" (Exod 20:14). They said to Him: *ervah* (illicit relations) is our entire essence, as it says, "And the two daughters of Lot conceived by their father" (Gen 19:36). He went to the children of Yishmael and said to them: Will you accept the Torah? They said: What is written in it? He said: "You shall not steal" (Exod 20:15). They said: Their entire essence, their father (i.e. Yishmael) is a brigand as it says, "And he (Yishmael) shall be a wild man, his hand against all" (Gen 16:12). And so to each and every nation, he asked them if they would accept the Torah, as it says, "All the kings of the earth will acknowledge You, God, for they heard the words of Your mouth" (Ps 138:4). Might it be that they heard and accepted? It is, therefore, taught saying, "And with anger and wrath will I take revenge of the nations because they did not hear" (Mic 5:14). It is not enough that they did not accept (hear) but even the seven commandments that the sons of Noah took upon themselves they could not abide by, until they divested themselves of them. Then the Holy One gave them to Israel. A parable: To one who sent his ass and his dog to the threshing floor, loading his ass with a *lethech* (= 15 *se'ah*) and his dog with three *se'ah*. The ass went and the dog panted, whereupon he took a *se'ah* from it and put it on the ass; and so with the second (*se'ah*) and so with the third. So, too, Israel accepted the Torah with all of its explanations and inferences; and even the seven commandments that the sons of Noah could not abide by until they divested themselves of them and Israel came and received them, therefore it says, "And he said: God came from Sinai, etc."

It is abundantly clear that even in tannaitic times, there was a strong particularist, even anti-Gentile view. In an interesting essay on this tannaitic source in the Sifre and its parallel in the Mekhilta and later versions, Shoval Shafat suggests that one can see editorial interventions in the Mekhilta—one that Shafat attributes to the last stages of editing of the tannaitic work in the early amoraic period. These editorial interventions were intended to move the source away from its universalistic tendencies.[6] So, too, this is possibly the case with our source in the Sifre. His thesis is well argued and persuasive, and also dovetails with the disappearance of universalistic tendencies in the amoraic period, but I am hesitant to accept the premise that these editorial interventions can or should be dated to the last stages of the editing of the work. Steven Fraade pointed out almost forty years ago that our Sifre passage and its preceding passages (the Torah was given from four directions and in four languages) have the shared refrain "When God was revealed to give the Torah to Israel." This indicates, in Fraade's reading, that all along the intent was to give the Torah to Israel, albeit in four major languages (Hebrew, Roman, Arabic, and Aramaic). I will focus on one line of this source, of anonymous authorship, and try to locate the named source behind it. Our source concludes the various offers of the Torah to different nations with the following summary:

> And so to each and every nation, he asked them if they would accept the Torah, as it says "All the kings of the earth will acknowledge You, God, for they heard the words of Your mouth" (Ps 138:4).

This midrash resolves the problem raised by this verse in Psalms by saying, yes, the nations of the world heard the revelation, but they did not accept it. This is a neat play on the two meanings of *"shema"* in Hebrew, to hear but also to obey or accept.[7] This same verse from Psalms appears in a comment in the Mekhilta attributed to R. Nathan, a late second-century/early third-century tanna. His comment is as follows:

> "You saw that from the heavens I spoke to you" (Exod 20:19)
> There is a difference between a person who sees, to others telling

that person. When others tell a person, sometimes the person's heart is divided; but here—"You saw!"

R. Nathan says: "You saw" (Exod 20:19) Why was this said? Since it says, "All the kings of earth will acknowledge you, O Lord, for they have heard the words of Your mouth," (Ps 138:4). It might be that just as they heard, so, they saw? (Scripture) teaches saying "You saw," but the nations of the world did not see.

(Mekhilta of Rabbi Yishmael, Yitro, tractate Baḥodesh, 9)

It is clear that already by the end of the second century the verse from Psalms 138 was understood to indicate that all of humanity heard God's voice, specifically at the Sinaitic revelation—"for they have heard the words of Your mouth." R. Nathan claims that Israel was privileged by seeing as well as hearing. The famous aggadah in the Sifre, cited above, adds all the nations of the world as having been approached to receive the Torah, not only Edom, Ishmael, and Moab, on the basis of that same Psalm verse according to R. Nathan's interpretation. The cosmic nature of revelation can be used both to universalize the giving of Torah but no less to discriminate and limit its reception to Israel only.

But why did this universal aspect all but disappear in amoraic times? Why was the vision of a united world under the God of Israel stored away until messianic times? We can only speculate. I will advance two possibilities that seem likely to me.

The first explanation is that the traditions and attitudes of R. Akiva predominated in amoraic times. His particularist approach overwhelmed what appears to have been the more universalist approach of his contemporary R. Yishmael. The second possibility is that the Christian adoption of universality and worldwide conversion as a measure for veracity, as evidenced in Justin Martyr's mid-second-century *Dialogue with Trypho*, caused the Jewish sages to shun the universalist approach. Let's explore both possibilities.

The assumption that R. Akiva's legal decisions prevailed in early amoraic times has been expressed in scholarly circles[8] and stands to reason as the bulk of the Mishna itself follows R. Akiva and his students.[9] Shmuel Safrai remarks that the norms of aggadah were not fixed with the same decisiveness as halacha, but Safrai goes on to opine still Akiva's influence in aggadah was "beyond a doubt" great. This then might explain the decisive turn to particularism, as an internal theological development due to the overpowering legacy of R. Akiva, his school, and its legacy.

Another possibility is to seek out historical reasons, including currents of thought in Christianity and the regnant cultures with which the Jewish sages came into contact. The mid-second-century Christian apologist Justin Martyr inveighs against Trypho the Jew in his *Dialogue with Trypho*, claiming Malachi's prophecy that "My name is great among the Gentiles, and in every place incense is offered to My name" is now fulfilled by the Christian Eucharist, whereas the Jewish sacrifices are in desuetude.[10] Might amoraic Judaism have abandoned universalist aspirations in the wake of these historical claims of the Christians? It would seem that the amoraic particularist turn preceded the formal recognition of Christianity in the Roman Empire of the fourth century. Were the second-century Christian apologists' claims sufficient to quash the universalist tendencies in tannaitic literature? I should think not, but I hesitate to leave it at that. For the Talmud itself declares that the recitation of the Ten Commandments in the daily liturgy was aborted due to the claims of the heretics, however we identify them. We see there Talmudic literature's self-awareness to what extent the Jewish sages were willing to go to combat errant beliefs.

At the turn of the fourth century CE, Eusebius asserts the triumph of Christianity in strikingly similar terms:

> For, since the doctrine of our Saviour has obtained throughout the whole creation of man, in every city, village, and place; and again, since no race of demons, but He alone who is the King of

all, God, and that creator of the whole world, the Word of God, has been made known and honoured by all men, Barbarians and Greeks; every word about fate has been rendered unavailing: every war-making necessity too has been removed far away: the Divine peace-making Word is hymned throughout the whole earth: the race of man is reconciled to God its Father; and peace and love have been restored to all nations![11]

Simmons, with whom we opened this chapter, has presented a convincing argument that the crisis of the Roman Empire in the third century was one of the contributing factors to the intellectual effort by Porphyry the philosopher, and even some of the third-century Roman emperors, to create and portray a universalist Roman religion. Porphyry gained good knowledge of Christianity possibly, according to Simmons and many others, in his studies with Origen in Caesarea. Porphyry, according to this view, attempts to counter the burgeoning gains of the universalist Christianity. The latter half of the third century was a period of relative peace for Christianity initiated by the emperor Gallienus (253–268), in which Christianity gained enormous popularity, owing to its message of universal salvation, as well as, according to Simmons, to its economic appeal in a time of economic crisis. Expensive animal sacrifices, at the core of pagan worship, were made obsolete by the Christian message of belief in the Savior. In addition, Christianity was renowned, in the footsteps of Judaism, for caring for all the poor and needy, not just Christian adherents.[12] Porphyry attempted, according to Simmons, to combat the attraction of the Christian message and appeal, by developing a coherent three-tiered path of universal salvation, geared to different pagan audiences. Porphyry's impressive intellectual tour de force seems to have been "too little too late" and, as Simmons would have it, by Constantine's time the emperor had little choice but to consolidate and unify the empire under Christianity. Yet Porphyry's developed system of universal salvation and the formidable attack he mounted on Christianity made him Christianity's central foe and required rebuttal throughout the fourth century and into the fifth.

It would seem, then, that while the Christian and pagan declarations of universal salvation vied with one another, both in the Roman and Sassanian empires, the Jewish sages' approach was to remove themselves from this contest and retreat into Jewish particularism, leaving the universalist message in the wings until messianic times. These two possible explanations, together and separately, for the disappearance of universalist tendencies in amoraic literature—that is, R. Akiva's legacy,[13] on the one hand, and the Christian-pagan universalist debate, on the other hand— might advance our understanding of this trend in rabbinic thought that dominated Jewish thought possibly to our own time.

References

Berthelot, Katell (2018), "Rabbinic Universalism Reconsidered," *Jewish Quarterly Review* 108: 393–421, https://www.jstor.org/stable/10.2307/90025843.

Birnbaum, E. (2016). "Some Particulars about Universalism," in *Crossing Boundaries in Early Judaism and Christianity* (Leiden: Brill): 115–137. https://doi.org/10.1163/9789004334496_007.

Cover, Michael Benjamin (2016), "*Paulus als Yischmaelit?* The Personification of Scripture as Interpretive Authority in Paul and the School of Rabbi Ishmael," *Journal of Biblical Literature* 135, no. 3 (2016): 617–637, https://doi.org/10.15699/jbl.1353.2016.3094.

Friedman, Shamma (2010), "What Does Mt. Sinai Have to Do with the Sabbatical Year?" (Hebrew) *Sidra: A Journal for the Study of Rabbinic Literature* 24–25: 387–426, http://liebermaninstitute.org.

Hayes, Christine, ed. (2022), *The Literature of the Sages: A Re-Visioning* (Leiden: Brill).

Hirshman, Marc (1999), *Torah for the Entire World—A Universalist Approach in Rabbinic Thought* (Hebrew) (Tel Aviv: Hakibbutz Hameuchad).

Hirshman, Marc (2000), "Rabbinic Universalism in the Second and Third Centuries," *Harvard Theological Review* 92: 101–115.

Levenson, Jon D. (1996), "The Universal Horizon of Biblical Particularism," in Dana de Priest (ed.), *Ethnicity and the Bible* (Leiden: Brill): 143–169.

Martyr, Justin, translated by Thomas B. Falls (1965), *The First Apology, The Second Apology, Dialogue with Trypho, Exhortation to the Greeks, Discourse to the Greeks, The Monarchy or The Rule of God* (Washington, DC: Catholic University of America Press).

Mirsky, Yehudah (2011), "Aqiva: Liberal, Existentialist, Prophet—Finkelstein, Heschel, Martin Luther King and Jewish Socio-Theological Thought in Mid-20th Century America," (Hebrew) *Daat: A Journal of Jewish Philosophy & Kabbalah* 71: 93–104, https://www.jstor.org/stable/24233072.

Safrai, Shmuel (1970), *Akiba* (Hebrew) (Jerusalem: Mosad Bialik).

Sandberg, Ruth N. (2017), "Rethinking the Notion of Universality in Judaism and Its Implications," *Studies in Christian-Jewish Relations* 12: 1–8.

Segal, Alan F. (1995), "Universalism in Judaism and Christianity," in Troels Engberg-Pedersen (ed.), *Paul in His Hellenistic Context* (Minneapolis: Fortress Press): 1–29.

Shafat, Shoval (2014), "The Legend about Offering the Torah to the Nations of the World and Its Alternative in the Tannaitic Midrashim and Amoraic Homilies from the Land of Israel," (Hebrew) *Hebrew Union College Annual* 84–85: 1–28, https://www.jstor.org/stable/10.15650/hebruniocollannu.84-85.1h?seq=1&cid=pdf-reference#references_tab_contents.

Simmons, Michael Bland (2015), *Universal Salvation in Late Antiquity: Porphyry of Tyre and the Pagan-Christian Debate.* (Oxford: Oxford University Press), https://academic.oup.com/book/2471.

Weinfeld, Moshe (1964), "Universalism and Particularism in the Period of Exile and Restoration," (Hebrew) *Tarbiz* 33: 228–242, https://www.jstor.org/stable/23591024.

Wilfand Ben Shalom, Yael (2014), *Poverty, Charity and the Image of the Poor in Rabbinic Texts from the Land of Israel* (Sheffield: Sheffield Phoenix Press).

Wilfand Ben Shalom, Yael (2017), *The Wheel That Overtakes Everyone: Poverty and Charity in the Eyes of the Sages* (Hebrew) (Tel Aviv: Hakkibutz Hameuchad).

Wright, Wilmer Cave (1923), *The Works of the Emperor Julian*, vol. 3 (Cambridge, MA and London: Harvard University Press, Loeb Classics).

Zlotnick, Dov (1988), *The Iron Pillar Mishna* (Jerusalem: Bialik Institute).

10

"This Is My Lord and I Will Glorify"

Rabbinic Religiosity

If I were asked what is one of my favorite passages in rabbinic literature of late antiquity, I would respond with the text we are about to study in this final chapter. It is taken from the mid-third-century tannaitic midrash on Exodus, called the Mechilta of R. Yishmael. This particular homily/exegesis is a long and fascinating interpretation of the second verse from the Song at the Sea (Exod 15:2): "The Lord is *my* strength and might; He is become *my* salvation. This is *my* God and *I* will enshrine Him ("extol Him"[1]), the God of *my* father and *I* will exalt Him" (NJPS, italics added). I have emphasized in bold the sixfold repetition of "I" and "my," reflecting an intimacy and possessiveness the people of Israel feel in this passage toward their God who has delivered them from the hands of the Egyptians. This triumphal poem goes on to talk of the devastation of the enemy and the deliverance of Israel, who are to be brought to God's holy place (*neve kodshekha*).[2] Surprisingly, the tannaitic reflection on this song introduces a universalist reprise, within the framework of God's deliverance of the "chosen people":

> (Exod 15:2) "and He was my salvation": You are a salvation unto all who enter the world, but unto me, more so.[3]

Yes, Israel has a privileged place in their relationship with God, as made clear in the Song at the Sea, but the midrash hastens to remind the readers that God is the God of all who come into the world and God will deliver them also. What was an atavistic victory song has been nuanced theologically. I have written elsewhere on this universalist strain of rabbinic thinking.[4] We will see that this universalism is upended later in our text. The interpretations of Exodus 15:2 begin with R. Eliezer's pronouncement that all present at the sea were granted a clear vision of God, surpassing that of the great later prophets.

> (10)[5] "This is my God": R. Eliezer says: Whence do you say that a maid-servant at the Red Sea saw what was not seen by Isaiah and Ezekiel, as it says, "And by the hand of the prophets I use similes" (Hos 12:11), and "The heavens were opened and I saw visions of God" (Ezek 1:1)? A parable (to what is this similar), to a king of flesh and blood who enters a province, with a circle of guards who surround him, warriors at his right and at his left, soldiers before him and behind him—and all were asking, "Who is the king?" For he is flesh and blood as they are. But when the Holy One was revealed on the sea, there was no need for anyone to ask, "Which is He?" For when they saw Him, they recognized Him, and they all opened (their mouths) and said, "This is my God, and I will extol Him."

R. Eliezer's opening statement asserts that all who were present at the sea pointed to their God with immediate recognition and said, "*This* is my God." Daniel Boyarin published a wonderful analysis of this passage, emphasizing R. Eliezer's interpretation of the word "this" as deictic, pointing.[6] The next six interpretations of the word *ve'anvehu* in the following passages of the Mechilta constitute for me a remarkable display of what second-century Jewish sages deemed to be the essence of religious behavior, each according to his own predilection[7]:

> (11) R. Yishmael says: Is it possible for flesh and blood to be beautiful before one's Creator?[8] Rather, "I shall beautify myself to

Him with the commandments—I will make before Him a beautiful palm branch (*lulav*), a beautiful booth (*sukka*), beautiful fringes (*tzitzit*), a beautiful phylactery *(tefilla)*.

Abba Shaul says: liken (yourself) to Him (*"ve'anvehu"* = *ani vehu* ["I and He"][9]) "Just as He is merciful and gracious, you, too, be merciful and gracious."

(12) R. Yose says: "[I will say][10] the beauty and praise of the One who spoke and the world was [before all the nations of the world]."[11]

R. Yose of Damascus says: "I shall make a beautiful Temple before Him," for *"na'eh"*[12] is nothing other than the Temple, as in (Ps 79:7) "and they have destroyed His Temple (*navehu*)," and (Isa 33:20) "Your eyes will see Jerusalem, as a secure homestead" (*naveh sha'anan*).

(13) R. Akiva says: "I shall speak of the beauty[13] and praise of the Holy One Blessed be He (other manuscripts: The One who spoke and brought the world into being) before all the nations of the world.

The nations of the world ask Israel: "How is your Beloved (better) than a beloved that you adjure us so? (Song 5:9) That you die for Him in this way and are murdered for Him in this way as it says, 'the maidens (*alamot*) have loved You' (Song 5:9)—they have loved You until death (*"al mot"*), and it is written (Ps 44:23) 'it is for Your sake we are slain all day long?' You are comely, you are strong. Come and join us."

(14) And Israel says to the nations of the worlds: "Do you know Him? Shall we tell you part of His praise (Song 5:10) 'My Beloved is clear skinned and ruddy, preeminent among ten thousand.'"

(15) When the nations of the world hear part of[14] the praise of the One who spoke and the world came into being, they say to Israel: "Let us go with you" (cf. Zech 8:23)[15] 'Whither has your beloved gone, O fairest of women? Whither has your beloved turned? Let us seek Him with you' (Song 6:1).

And Israel says to them 'My beloved is mine, and I am his' (Song 2:16), and 'I am my beloved's, and my beloved is mine, He browses among the lilies'" (Song 6:3).

(16) And the sages say: I shall accompany Him ("*alavenhu*")[16] until I come with Him to His Temple... and so it says, "scarcely had I passed them when I found the one I love. I held him fast, I would not let go till I brought him to my mother's house, to the chamber of her who conceived me" (Song 3:4).

The sages' view is amplified by a parable of a king following and protecting his son in the latter's peregrinations, which I have omitted here. The passage ends looking to the future—again quoting the Song of Songs with God and Israel being united and restored to house and chamber—rendered elsewhere as the tabernacle and the Temple.[17]

This I understand to be the completion of the exegesis begun with R. Eliezer and culminating in the six understandings of *ve'anvehu*.[18] It is to the religious attitudes contained in these six interpretations that we will now turn our focus. Let us begin with the first two. R. Yishmael stresses the distance between God and human beings. Humans, he holds, are incapable of "adding" to God's beauty (*na'eh*). The most a human can do is fulfill God's commandments in a beautiful way and, thus in some oblique way, beautify what God had decreed. One glorifies God by adding luster to God's commandments rather than to Godself. The next sage, Abba Shaul moves in a wholly different direction, shrinking the gap between the divine and the human. He understands "glorifying" (*ve'anvehu*) as being like God, together with God (*ani vehu*),[19] imitating God's divine traits of graciousness and mercy. If God is perfect in glory, the essence of that glory is God's traits of mercy and graciousness that a human can adopt and imitate.[20]

In these first two interpretations, we have the first sage assuming the incommensurability of God, while second sage stresses the accessibility of God's attributes. The one chooses elegant adherence to the commandments, while the other strives for human perfection of values. These are two quite different stances as to what constitutes the pinnacle of religious behavior. The next and third interpretation speaks of declaring God's praise to be the fulfillment of *ve'anvehu*. This is the religious sentiment that lies behind many of the Psalms and all nonpetitionary prayer. One glorifies God by singing God's praises.

It is R. Yose from Damascus who suggests that the fulfillment of *ve'anvehu* is to build God's sanctuary. This interpretation amalgamates the two understandings of *na'eh*, beauty, and *naveh*, a dwelling, into a single interpretation—building a beautiful temple. God's glory ultimately is to be found at its most sacred, neither in God's commandments nor in God's traits but rather in God's real presence in the Temple. The verse instructs the Jewish people, according to this view, to build a beautiful temple. We emphasize that this interpretation is from the mouth of a second century sage who lived a half century or more after the Temple's destruction in 70 CE. This is another indication of some of the sages' firm belief that the restoration was imminent and the Temple would be rebuilt, if not within the seventy-year span of the First Temple, then not long after.

All of the above lead us to R. Akiva, who also calls for praising God before the nations of the world. In the order the Mechilta has chosen to present the interpretations, R. Akiva's interpretation seems to be a repetition of his student R. Yose's interpretation.[21] What distinguishes R. Akiva is the extraordinary Scriptural dialogue that presents itself as the continuation of R. Akiva's statement.[22] This brilliant and elegant midrash turns the dialogue in the Song between the beloved and the daughters of Jerusalem, into a dialogue between Israel and the nations of the world.[23] The intertwining of Eros and Thanatos, Love and Death, has been noted and wonderfully explicated by Daniel Boyarin. I quote his summary:

The midrash represents the relationship of God and the Jewish people as an erotic one—through the reading of Song of Songs into Exodus. However, Thanatos also introduces itself into this erotic idyll—formally and thematically.[24]

No less striking, but generally neglected by scholarship, is the exclusivity of R. Akiva's vision here. He paints a picture of God's beauty for the nations, but as soon as they are enthralled and won over, he summarily rebuffs them—God and Israel are lovers in an exclusive relationship that will permit no third party. As Alan Mintz remarked:

> But the answer returns: "I am my Beloved's and my Beloved is mine!" The diad [sic] is inviolable; at some level God's grace extends to all the world, but the mystery of the loving mutuality between God and Israel must of necessity render the relationship between Israel and the nations in terms of irremediable exclusivity.[25]

How are we to construe R. Akiva's glorifying God before the nations while at the same time rejecting their bid to accompany Israel in this love affair? Does this mean that R. Akiva demanded conversion before joining in Israel's relationship, or was this an outright rejection of non-Jews worshipping and adoring God? Was this a mission to the Gentiles or was it aimed entirely for internal consumption?

I fear that I have no definitive answer to these questions. Rather, I wish to highlight R. Akiva's view and contrast it with the opening section of the Mechilta above. There we saw that the Mechilta went out of its way, despite the resounding tones of a national victory song, to emphasize God's universality— "You are a salvation *unto all who enter the world*, but unto me, more so." This contrasts starkly to the allegorical reading of the Song of Songs by R. Akiva that turned it into a paean to Jewish particularism, rejecting the nations altogether.

This Mechilta source provides us with the opportunity to reflect on the variety of religious options available to the learner. God can be praised through elegant ritual, through ethical behavior, through a holy site, through praise itself, and through missionizing, impressing others with God's special love for Israel. Is the best way to glorify God through adherence to God's commandments or through emulating God's traits? Is the pinnacle of Judaism restoring the Temple or describing God's beauty to the nations?

Some may prefer to read the six interpretations as complementing one another. My own view is that rabbinic thought preferred diversity and left it up to the individual adherent or the community to form priorities. This flexibility allowed for a unity in learning the same sources but great diversity in practice.

We have seen throughout our study that rabbinic literature exults in debate and controversy. Mystics and legalists, aggadists and poets, found their place together offering diverse models for what was the best way to serve God in this world. The mainstream of rabbinic thought opted for Torah study as the focus of the religion, but there was ample room within the tradition of debate for strikingly other visions of piety. This flexibility of the religious outlook surely accounts for the richness of the varying visions and their tenacity though the centuries.

References

Bar-Or Melchior, Shira (2011), "Who Spoke and the World Was" (Hebrew), Master's thesis, Hebrew University of Jerusalem.
Boyarin, Daniel (1990), *Intertextuality and the Reading of Midrash* (Bloomington: Indiana University Press).
Boyarin, Daniel (1999), *Dying for God: Martyrdom and the Making of Christianity and Judaism* (Stanford, CA: Stanford University Press).
Chadwick, Henry (1959), *The Sentences of Sextus: A Contribution to The History of Early Christian Ethics* (Cambridge: Cambridge University Press).

Goldin, Judah (1990), *The Song at the Sea: Being a Commentary on a Commentary in Two Parts* (Philadelphia: The Jewish Publication Society).

Hirshman, Marc (2000), "Rabbinic Universalism in the Second and Third Centuries," *Harvard Theological Review* 92: 101–115.

Horovitz, H.S. and I. A. Rabin (1970), *Mechilta D'Rabbi Ismael* (Jerusalem: Wahrmann).

Kahana, Menahem (2018), "The Good in the Sight of Heaven and Right in the Sight of Man," *Tarbiz* 85: 557–586, https://www.jstor.org/stable/26873772.

Lewy, Israel (1876), "Ueber Einige Fragmente Aus Der Mischna Des Abba Saul," *Zweiter Bericht Über Die Hochschule Für Die Wissenschaft Des Judenthums in Berlin* 2: 3–36.

Marmorstein, Arthur (1950), *Studies in Jewish Theology* (Oxford: Oxford University Press).

Mintz, Alan (1981), "The Song at the Sea and the Question of Doubling in Midrash," *Prooftexts* 1: 185–192, https://www.jstor.org/stable/20689001.

Rosen-Zvi, Ishay (2008), "Can the Homilists Cross the Sea Again? Revelation in Mekhilta Shirata," in George Brooke et al. (eds.), *The Significance of Sinai: Traditions about Sinai and Divine Revelation in Judaism and Christianity* (Leiden: Brill): 217–245, https://brill.com/view/title/15240.

Epilogue
Why Study Late Antique Judaism

In the last quarter of the twentieth century, the Western canon of classical literature began to lose its traction in college curricula in favor of diverse ethnic and gender-oriented courses. The study of late antiquity continued to be popular though, a field recently reinvigorated by its new name, Late Antiquity, and the stellar research of its practitioners, Peter Brown in the forefront, and many others such as Robin Lane Fox. Suddenly this period between the second and sixth centuries CE was no longer seen as a period of decline, as Edward Gibbon had famously characterized it, but rather as the bedrock of Western civilization in general and Christianity more specifically. At the same time, the "literary turn," a new perspective on the literary aspects of these historical sources, supplanted the elusive pursuit of the historical kernel of ancient literature. These trends had a profound effect on Jewish studies in general and on the study of midrash and Talmud more specifically. Specialists arose in the literary analysis of midrash and aggadah in Israel and abroad, such as Zipporah Kagan, Ofrah Meir, and Yonah Fraenkel, Renee Bloch, Judah Goldin, David Stern, Daniel Boyarin, Steven Fraade, James Kugel, Menahem Kister, Joshua Levinson and many others. In addition, folklore scholars, such as Raphael Patai, Haim Schwarzbaum, and Dov Noy and his students, especially Galit Hasan Rokem, made important advances, with Louis Ginzberg's magnificent contributions serving as the great compendium of the Legends of the Jews.

While these literary currents sparked a growth in the humanities in general, Jewish studies in general and rabbinic literature more specifically grew exponentially. For example, from a modest beginning of a handful of chairs in the United States at mid-century, with most of the research still being done in theological seminaries, by the end of the century, chairs in Talmud and midrash were established in scores of universities. At the same time, the non-academic study of Talmud, whether in Yeshivot, especially in Israel, or by laypeople in the ever more popular *daf-yomi* cycle, reached an audience the size of which its late antique creators, one suspects, would never dare to imagine. Why this attraction to rabbinic literature both in the format of midrash and even more so in the Babylonian Talmud itself?

I would like to think this through with you from a number of angles. To start, most of the Jewish sages of late antiquity, but not all, gave study and learning pride of place. In this they continued the nascent agenda of the book of Deuteronomy, but the passion with which the study of the Oral Torah was promoted by these sages was determinative. Written Torah was venerated, while Oral Torah became the focus of advanced learning. This tradition of learning for learning's sake certainly shaped the character of the Jewish people for generations, possibly until our own times.

While tannaitic literature was produced in the orbit of Roman Palestine and a surging Christian movement, amoraic literature began integrating the Aramaic vernacular, both in Palestine and Babylonia, along with the more scholarly Hebrew. The early generations of sages of the Jerusalem Talmud and the Babylonian Talmud carried on a long-distance relationship, while surely the religious and social norms of Sassanian Iraq were often quite different from those of Roman Palestine. The sages somehow carried on a conversation across borders of competing empires and competing cultures. Thus, while Hellenistic thought and Christianity did, according to many modern scholars, also influence Babylonian Jewry, the two Talmuds and the Land of Israel midrashic corpus comprise a mirror of a wide swath of ancient culture, Eastern and Western.

At the same time one is amazed that the same sages who employed a "hyper-deductive" method, as Harry Austryn Wolfson called it, in their discussion of matters legal, from the most arcane to the everyday, were the same rabbis who engaged in the most fanciful aggadic exegesis and composed surrealistic legends. The great Babylonian sage Rav seats Moses in R. Akiva's classroom, while the Land of Israel sages talk of the manna climbing to a height of 150 cubits. One of the Talmudic sages is reported to have leaped into the World to Come, while still alive, without permission.

How and why should one navigate the more than 2,700 folio pages of the Babylonian Talmud and the vast legal and aggadic midrash on the five books of Moses and some of the other biblical books? Let us begin with why and answer in brief with three reasons: perspective, perspicacity, and playfulness. The Talmud and the midrash model, in a most singular fashion, the ability to approach a problem from multiple perspectives. Sometimes the analyses lead to a whittling down of perspective, but more often than not, especially in aggadic midrash, one is asked to retain the various perspectives, though they often conflict. All literary works up until and through the Middle Ages show humans grappling with universal problems but in physical and social circumstances vastly different from ours. This provides the contemporary reader with a sounding board for one's own thoughts. Rabbinic literature does the same for its students. Finally, oral works, later committed to writing, attest to a human capacity to absorb and retain vast amounts of knowledge, a capacity seriously impacted in our computer age. When I see a great musician playing an intricate work by heart and when I recall Professor Lieberman's astounding memory feats, I can imagine that it was possible to retain the oral law in its oral nature.

Like all great works of antiquity, the insights of wise people are treasured and handed down from generation to generation. Rabbinic literature not only treasured sayings of the wise but insisted on retaining their pedigree as far as humanly possible.

It was vital, according to the Talmud, to both enchain a received saying to at least three generations and even more so to visualize the sage who had taught the adage. Certainly, the method of argumentation of the Talmudic sages has left its imprint on Jewish culture but no less so has the flight of exegetical imagination around Scripture, leaving its indelible imprint on the Nobel Prize–winning author S. Y. Agnon. This combination of disciplined argumentation alongside verbal acrobatics stimulates the contemporary student and challenges one on many levels. Perspicacity engages all readers and prods them to deeper thinking.

Finally, rabbinic literature beginning with its oral roots in schools and synagogues is all too human in its playfulness, even sometimes overdoing it. One sage opened every session with a joke, while some of the aggadic flights of fancy were clearly meant to entertain. Like ancient rhetoric, its Jewish counterpart aggadah (both meaning speaking) were designed to entertain and persuade. Aggadic literature was characterized by one of its practitioners as "tugging at one's heart."

Nineteenth-century Jewish intellectuals sometimes distanced themselves from the overly pedantic and picayune nature of Talmudic discussion. The ancient sages themselves were cognizant that sometimes borders were crossed and the inquiry had gone too far—epitomized in the impatient reaction to R. Jeremiah's doting questions on legal borderline situations. He cast doubt on the very ability to quantify distances and measures in legal cases. In the nonlegal context, great sages were sometimes reprimanded for being too fanciful or audacious in their aggadic interpretations.

Much has been said from the nineteenth century through our own times about how, for the Jewish people, the Bible and rabbinic literature became their homeland after the second destruction of the Temple. Certainly the intense study of the Bible, Mishna, and rabbinic literature, along with the Hebrew prayers and poetry composed in late antiquity, went a long way to both sustain the Jewish people's fealty to the Hebrew language and facilitate its revival in the twentieth century as a spoken language.

It would be grossly negligent not to acknowledge that rabbinic literature is a product of its time, authored by males from an anthropocentric perspective. The last fifty years have witnessed a wonderful corrective, in feminist readings of Talmud by the first generation of female scholars, such as Judith Hauptman, Shulamit Valler, Tal Ilan, Vered Noam, Devora Steinmetz, and many, many others. The Talmud and midrash, owing to what I have called grounded spirituality, earthy spirituality, also made room for non-rabbinic voices that are echoed by the rabbis, reflecting everyday life of their times, including artisans and doctors, women and children, even competing religions and heretical voices.

But, for me, the main reason to spend time with these oral, now written, works of the Jewish sages of the first six centuries of the Common Era is their energetic adoption of conflicting points of view and their ability to accommodate them without harmonizing them. The Talmud raised a protest against the book of Ecclesiastes since its reputed author, Solomon, not only contradicted his father, David, but also contradicted himself. But as one of my teachers remarked often, nobody ever died of a contradiction. The heart of the lesson that runs through all of rabbinic literature is the knowledge that life is shot through with contradictions. Real wisdom is to be able to hold on to conflicting views and apply each one in its proper time and place. Living with Talmudic learning, especially when so much emphasis has been placed on memory, affords one the tools to meet real-life situations with a depth and strength rarely surpassed. I recall that George Steiner once wrote that he never interpreted a poem until he had committed it to memory. This remains the gold standard of study of rabbinic literature, though computers and artificial intelligence have mounted a spirited assault. Rabbinic literature remains a goldmine of human musings and argumentation along with striking ethical and theological reflections. Its study is as rewarding today as it was almost two thousand years ago. Its study will enhance one's wisdom while nurturing at the same time incredulity toward those claiming absolute truths. It is well worth the immense effort needed to engage it.

Notes

Chapter 1

1. See, for example, Samuel Hugo Bergmann's reflections on the system of blessings developed by the Sages in Samuel Hugo Bergmann, "On Blessings," in *People and Ways: Philosophical Journeys* (Hebrew) (Jerusalem: Bialik, 1967): 387–391.
2. Yaakov Sussman, *Oral Law—Taken Literally: The Power of the Tip of a Yod* (Hebrew) (Jerusalem: Magnes 2019) is the definitive statement on this issue; Martin S. Jaffee, *Torah in the Mouth: Writing and Oral Tradition in Palestinian Judaism, 200 BCE–400 CE* (Oxford: Oxford University Press, 2001).
3. Shamma Friedman, "The Primacy of Tosefta to Mishnah in Synoptic Parallels," in *Introducing Tosefta: Textual, Intratextual and Intertextual Studies* (1999): 99–121. This is an accessible English presentation of Friedman's extensive Hebrew research on the subject.
4. See M. Kahana, "The Halakhic Midrashim," in S. Safrai et al., *The Literature of the Sages* (Assen: Royal Van Gorcum Fortress Press, 2006): 3–106.
5. David Halivni and Jeffrey Rubenstein, ed. and trans., *The Formation of the Babylonian Talmud* (New York: Oxford University Press, 2013).
6. Jacob Neusner raised the question early on; see his "Evaluating the Attributions of Sayings to Named Sages in the Rabbinic Literature," *Journal for the Study of Judaism in the Persian, Hellenistic, and Roman Period* 26, no. 1 (1995): 93–111.
7. Richard Lee Kalmin, *Jewish Babylonia between Persia and Roman Palestine* (Oxford: Oxford University Press, 2006), introduction and especially pp. 15–16.
8. See Megan Hale Williams's review essay of *No More Clever Titles: Observations on Some Recent Studies of Jewish-Christian Relations in the Roman World*, by Adam H. Becker, Annette Yoshiko Reed, Daniel Boyarin, and Judith M. Lieu, *The Jewish Quarterly Review* 99, no. 1 (2009): 37–55.
9. A. Cameron, *Dialoguing in Late Antiquity* (Cambridge: Cambridge University Press, 2014).
10. An earlier Hebrew version appeared in J. Hacker, ed., *Wise Hearted: The World of the Sages: Studies in Memory of Jaffa Hacker* (Hebrew) (Jerusalem: Mossad Bialik, 2017).

Chapter 2

1. I have adopted but liberally adapted Jeffrey Rubenstein's translation (Rubenstein 2010: 182–183). I am grateful for his careful translation. My additions, changes and omissions are to serve the analysis here.

2. bShabbat 89a; Songs Rabbah 8,10, etc.
3. Fraenkel (1977–1978): 157–172. Much has been written on the "jots and tittles," the crowns of the letters. In an incisive and learned essay, "The Script of the Torah in Rabbinic Thought (B): Transcriptions and Thorns" (Heb.) *Leshonenu* (2010): 89–123, Shlomo Naeh presented the case that "*kotz*" is to be understood not as the adornment of the letter but rather as a section of Torah "*kotza*." Though his is a solid case given the parallel in Songs Rabbah, in our context, I still maintain, as do many others, that the reference is to the crowns of the letter to which R Akiva was able to attach significance. Naeh is, of course, correct that we have no such derashot, but I don't think that Rav in his storytelling refrained from hyperbole. See further Yakir Paz, "'Binding Crowns to the Letters'—A Divine Scribal Practice in Its Historical Context" (Heb.), *Tarbiz* 86 (2019): 233–268 (and ample bibliography about the story in n. 4) who took Naeh's insight to a further level, suggesting that this passage reflects the scribal practice of a "coronis" that signified the end of a paragraph or a book. Both of these gifted scholars brought significant findings to support their interpretations, but, as Paz noted, the Bavli editor ends the story with Rava's comment about the seven letters in the Torah that are decorated, clearly showing how the editor understood the original story. Paz's remonstration that Rava, a few generations after the storyteller Rav, is the first to note this decoration does not close the door on the possibility that this was an older tradition and scribal practice.
4. Alternately, the word "immediately" (*miyad*) may be read at the end of the previous sentence, "you should have helped me immediately" and followed by Moses's reply, "he said."
5. Rosenthal (2021): 769.
6. Heschel (2005): 552–564; Halivni (1991): 113ff.; B. Sommer, *Revelation and Authority: Sinai in Jewish Scripture and Tradition* (New Haven, CT: Yale University Press, 2015), chapter 2.
7. Rosenthal (2021): 739–792.
8. S. Naeh, "The Structure and Division of Torat Kohanim (A): Scrolls" (Hebrew), *Tarbiz* 66 (1997): 483–515, especially 496ff. See Kister (2021).
9. Antiquities 13:297 along with M. Jaffee, *Torah in the Mouth* (New York: Oxford University Press, 2001): 51–52.
10. Boyarin (2019).
11. Urbach (1947): 7, 10.
12. Translated in Lieberman (1962): 207. The bracketed translation seems to be a summary of the literal rhetorical question and response: "which is that? The Mishna given orally."
13. Ibid., p. 208. Zussman (2005) argued that the oral Torah wasn't written at all, and his view was generally accepted.
14. Tanchuma Tisa 16, cited by Halivni (1991): 113.

Chapter 3

1. See Greenwood (2021: 102), who endorses the view that Epistle 22 is authentic.
2. Julian (1923: 71).
3. It also stands in stark contrast to Martial's first-century view of the Jewish beggar. Stern (1974: 1.529) and his reference in note 1 to H. J. Lewy, *Studies in Jewish Hellenism* (Hebrew) (Jerusalem: Mosad Bialik, 1960), 197ff.
4. Ruth Rabbah 2:14.

5. Leviticus Rabbah 34:2. The NJPS translates the verse as did the midrash: "He who is generous to the poor makes a loan to the Lord," as do the LXX and English translations.
6. Tob 12:8–9. See the nice quote of Tob 4:6–11 in Satlow (2010: 264), following Fitzmyer's translation: "To all those who practice righteousness give alms from what you have; and do not let your eye begrudge the giving of alms. Do not turn your face away from any poor person. Then God's face will not be turned away from you. According to what you have, give alms from it in proportion to your abundance; if you have little, do not be afraid to give the little you can. So you will be storing up good treasure for yourself against a day of need. For almsgiving preserves one from death and keeps one from going off into darkness. Indeed, almsgiving is a good gift in the sight of the Most High for all who give it." Satlow's fine essay takes as its starting point popular stories about charity in rabbinic literature and goes on to be a quite comprehensive review of the history of almsgiving in biblical and Second Temple times along with noting philological uses of equivalent terms for charity along with good comparison to Christian developments. I am less sure of his historical reconstruction, and I would not postpone rabbinic institutional development to the third or fourth centuries.
7. Sir 3:30 [Hebrew 3:28]. Cited also by Satlow (2010: 263). On this passage of Ben Sira and its context, see the illuminating note in Novick (2012: 42–43 n. 25), and Weinfeld's derivation of the term *gemillut ḥesed* cited there (Weinfeld 1995).
8. Present tense, subject undetermined. So, too, in the following translation "we" can also be "they."
9. For this translation and an insightful study of the term *parnas*, see Fraade (2011: 555–576).
10. Correcting *nun* to *tav*.
11. Sokoloff (1990: 229). Pnei Moshe commentary ad locum: "would explain and teach them words of Torah." Literally the phrase probably means "to load them with Torah."
12. Schwartz (2010: 131 n. 57).
13. See Fraade (2011: 558–569). Fraade, on p. 576 n. 60, references an excellent MA thesis written at the Hebrew University by Daniel Meir in 2007, entitled "The Parnas In Israel—Identity, Status and Authority," that came to his attention after he had completed his article. The thesis is a comprehensive and well-written treatment of both epigraphy and texts along with comparative material to similar positions in Roman Syria and Egypt.
14. Following Fraade (2011: 569).
15. "*misaken*"—Sokoloff (1990: 378) translates: "in mortal danger."
16. Translation based on Margulies (1993: 774–775).
17. Meir (2007: 46) raises two possibilities of this location near Tiberias and the people's reluctance to accept the position of *parnas*.
18. For this type of seating, see Simon Malmberg, "Visualising Hierarchy at Imperial Banquets," *Feast, Fast or Famine* (Leiden: Brill, 2017: 19).
19. See, for example, the beautiful mosaic from this period in a villa at Lod (Gorzalczany 2016).
20. Aramaic *knishta* is equivalent to the Greek *synagogue*. On this source and *euergetism* that Wilfand rightly notes also penetrated the rabbinic elite, see Wilfand (2017: 299–302 and especially note p. 301 n. 6).
21. Only in the Vienna manuscript of the Tosefta does it stipulate that he gave his stores to the poor as it does explicitly in the Jerusalem Talmud parallel in Pe'ah 1:1. The other witnesses of the Tosefta that do not read "for the poor" would be a good example of the classic *euergetes*, good works and generosity of the Roman nobility

toward the population in general! The Tosefta's version, even without the words "for the poor," turns the *euergetes* into charity for the poor by the verses added, each employing the root *zdk*. On *euergetism* and a fine treatment of some of the sources brought here, see Schwartz (2010: 129–135). For a comprehensive and penetrating view of this source and the differences between this and other rabbinic sources and *euergetism*, see Wilfand Ben Shalom (2014: 240–268).
22. Urbach (1980:117–124); Anderson (2013: 123–135). Anderson (2013: 128–129) treats possible Second Temple antecedents, Psalms of Solomon and later Second Baruch, that focus on good deeds and righteousness being stored in heaven.
23. B. Talmud Ketubot 67a, Rashi glossing the word *lihitparnes* as "food from charity." Compare Lieberman Tosefta Ki-fshuta Ketubot, p. 281, with a quote from geonic times that extends the priority of women to clothing and food, though that might be dealing with marital preparations. See also R. David Pardo in his *Hasdei David* commentary on Tosefta Horayot 2:6 where he cites Maimonides extending this preference to food also. Pardo himself demurs if the charity involved is actually a matter of life and death, in which case he thinks that again preference would be extended to the male.

Chapter 4

1. Sifra Kedoshim 4, 12.
2. Tomson (2015).
3. Winandy (1964).
4. Tomson (2015: 446).
5. Lawson (1957: 31).
6. Satran (2018: 39).
7. R. Simon ben Lakish was known to castigate Babylonians who gathered in groups when in the Land of Israel for not having made Aliya en masse when they should have (Song of Songs Rabbah 8:9 with a parallel b. Yoma 9b in a very different setting—again in the Jordan River as in b. Bava Metzi'a 84a).
8. Boyarin (1995: 198). He goes on to analyze the grotesque in Bakhtinian terms.
9. The nickname means "first and last" like "alpha omega" in Greek. See Wasserstein (1979).
10. Bacher (1892: 340), noting that he is never called a student of bar Kappara.
11. Bacher (1892: 344–345 n. 4) notes that I. H. Weiss and Graetz rejected the story.
12. Bacher (1892: 407): "Agadische künheiten."
13. In a wonderful and comprehensive Hebrew essay on R. Samuel Yaffe Ashkenazi (Benayahu 1973), Meir Benayahu surmised that this commentary was the biggest book published in Hebrew from the invention of printing to Benayahu's own times (p. 427)!
14. I use the word *soul* here, but it is important to bear in mind Jon Levenson's strictures on "nefesh"; *soul* in the Bible: "means one should love him with all one's vitality, vigor, energy, selfhood, inner forcefulness, and the like. It does not mean that one should love him with some immortal and spiritual dimension of the self that is divorced from one's bodily and social identity" (Levenson 2016: 70).
15. Rosen-Zvi (2011: 103).
16. Stern (1986: 121).
17. Aside from the proper name Ḥovav, Moses's father-in law (Num 10:29, Judg 4:11).
18. Compare Maharal's comment a thousand years later "that one cannot love two equally thus sometimes the learned are so enamored of Torah even more than

they are of its Giver." Maharal of Prague (Judah Loew ben Bezalel), *Tiferet Yisrael* (Hebrew) (Jerusalem: Machon Yerushalayim 2000): 45; and elsewhere in Maharal's writings.
19. yBerachot 5:1. See also bEruvin 54b. This is reminiscent of the philosopher Thales falling into a well while stargazing (Plato, Theaetetus 174a).
20. On identification of wisdom with Torah in Second Temple times and later, see Uusimäki (2014: 347-348).
21. Much has been written on martyrdom—*kiddush hashem*—as the pinnacle of love of God. See again Levenson (2016: 79ff and bibliography on 212 n. 34) and Fishbane (1996).
22. The saying continues: "no beauty like the beauty of Jerusalem, no wealth like the wealth of Rome, no might like the might of Persia, no lasciviousness like that of Arabia, no sorcery like the sorcery of Egypt."
23. I think the best translation is "talk" or "speech," but it is not to be found in any modern translation. LXX translates *melete*.
24. See Idel (2005: 31) for an analysis of the mystical context of this statement. Idel (258 n. 46) quotes Menahem Kasher as linking this statement with R. Akiva's view, as I also intimated here.

Chapter 5

1. Goldin (1965). See note 6 below.
2. Wolfson (1942).
3. Lieberman (1974: 222). Much has been written about Oenomaus. Now, see Joseph Geiger's stimulating article, "Why Oenomaus the Gaderene?" (Hebrew) in S. Naeh and Y. Rosenthal, *Mehqerei Talmud 4* (Jerusalem: Magnes Press, 2023): 13-201.
4. Harvey (1992: 84).
5. Hidary (2022: 330-335).
6. Goldin (1965). The Hebrew version of the essay that appeared around the same time had the more modest title of "Something of Rabban Yoḥanan ben Zakkai's Beit Midrash."
7. The best manuscripts of the Mishna (Kaufmann, Loewe, and Parma along with some Geniza fragments read *asita*—"if you've done." Though this formulation might also mean "learn." See Abramson (1953: 61-66).
8. Goldin translated the Hebrew idiom as "take no credit to thyself" and similarly Kulp. I tried to retain the overly literal translation to emphasize the word *tova* meaning "good" that returns in his question to his students.
9. I have used Joshua Kulp's translation at Sefaria, consulting also Goldin's translation and making several changes along the way.
10. Goldin (1965: 3).
11. This is the manuscript reading, whereas the printed editions which Goldin followed read *yeshara*, "straight" or right."
12. 1 Sam 12:23; 1 Kgs 8:36; Jer 6:16; 2 Chr 6:27. See also Isa 62:2.
13. The phenomenon of parallel questions and themes in Avot, of which this is only one example, warrants further research.
14. Goldin (1965: 19).
15. Epictetus, *Discourses*, 2.11.13.
16. Harvey (1992: 86).
17. There are ethical debates but generally short and to the point with little argumentation, for example, the long treatment of how to honor aged parents whose mental

126   NOTES

   faculties are impaired (bKiddusin 31b ff). For the view that rabbinic literature is philosophy, see, e.g., Fischel (1973); Neusner (2002).
18. Some wonderful examples of argumentation in the Mishna are m. Pesahim 6:1-5 and m. Yadayim 4:3-11.
19. Wilfand (2019, 2021); Furstenberg (2019); Malka (2019); Malka and Paz (2021).
20. Niehoff (2012); Paz (2022).
21. Hidary (2017); Novick (2012). See also Brodsky (2014).
22. Luz (1989).
23. Bickerman (1988).
24. See, for example, Kister (2013: 139 n. 28).
25. Shoval-Dudai (2019); Sperber (1984, 2012).
26. Rosenthal (2017).
27. Lieberman (1987: 157-225).
28. Hirshman (1988: 164ff).
29.   Schwartz and Tomson (2018) have recently argued that the anonymous *Liber Antiquitatum Biblicarum*, a rewriting of the biblical narrative, not unlike Josephus's *Antiquities*, belongs to the world of the rabbinic sages of the Yavne period.

Chapter 6

1. "Arayot," illicit relations, is also counted in that same Mishna, as a restricted field of study, though ostensibly with no connection to mysticism. Rather, it is restricted due to the intricacies and delicate nature of the subject. See Origen's reckoning below.
2. *kavod*—"glory, honor"—is a synonym from biblical times and on for God's presence.
3. The scholarly bibliography on this Mishna and rabbinic mysticism is legion.
4. I have translated "*ein dorshin*" as "*we* do not *teach*." Since the Mishna uses the usual participial form, it may be translated also as "they." So, too, *dorshin* is usually understood in terms of exegesis or homilies but can also be legal teaching (see Mandel 2017: 13-19). *Dorshin* here I think is teaching the midrash of these subjects.
5. Translating ms. Kaufman reading "*veheivin*." See discussion in Halbertal (2008: 8-11). Mandel (2017: 223 n. 5), in a long note gives an interesting alternative definition to "*veheivin midaato*" as "instructing" "with [his] permission." I remain convinced that in this Mishna and especially in light of the Tosefta story, it should be understood as "understood," though I think Mandel is correct that "*midaato*" should not be translated as "on his own" but possibly as "by one's own will," as he suggests.
6. *maaseh* here is very close to the Greek *chreia*, a short anecdote with a message with the Hebrew root meaning "do" akin to the Greek use.
7. Literally: "recount." See Mandel (2017: 238 n. 41). I prefer "lecture," which gives a better sense of the activity.
8. We have a strikingly similar account at t. Pesahim 2:16 (Lieberman, 147) of Rabban Gamliel alighting from his donkey, seating himself, and wrapping himself in a *tallit* in order to annul a vow. The Tosefta there goes on to state it as a rule: "we do not annul vows, neither riding, nor walking. Nor standing but wrapped and seated."
9. There is an alternate explanation that Halbertal (2008) lays out on pp. 10-11 but rightly says that the Tosefta precludes that explanation.
10. For select bibliography, see Mandel (2017: 223 n. 5) and Halperin (1980). Mandel prefers "instruction" (and especially teaching halacha) as the definition, but in our context, with the previous Mishna Hagiga 1:8 outlining the relation of the oral

Torah to Scripture (*mikra*), I think we should retain here the commonly accepted translation of *darash* meaning to interpret Scripture.
11. See Fraenkel (1977) for his expert analysis of those stories.
12. The verb *hmr* appears only in the Tosefta story, as opposed to the parallels in the Babylonian and Jerusalem Talmuds that have a more general prosaic term "walking after him." The verb only appears here and in a number of places in the Babylonian Talmud, but I suspect is original to the story, rather than the more pedestrian "walking after." For guiding donkeys with a two-pronged stick, "no bit was used for the mules' mouths, and sometimes no reins either: the animals were controlled by tapping them on the side with a two-pronged stick or whip" (Griffith 2006: 234 and see n. 166).
13. See note 3 above.
14. m. Kerithot 3:7 and parallels: R. Akiva asks a question of R. Joshua and Rabban Gamliel in the market (*atles*) of Emmaus relating to illicit relations performed unwittingly; m. Avodah Zarah 2:5: R. Yishmael asks R. Joshua about the prohibition of eating gentile cheese; Mechilta *Tisa* 1: three rabbis followed by two younger rabbis and a question was "asked before them" about saving a life that overrides the Sabbath.
15. T. Pe'ah 3:2; t. Hallah 1:6; t. Yoma 2:7; t. Me'ilah 1:5. At Mechilta Amalek Jethro 2, Jethro's advice to Moses that Moses should "bring the words/things" that God had told him to the people is rendered in the midrash, "things that you hear bring and recount/report to them."
16. The Tosefta commentary *Ḥazon Yeḥezkel* ad locum and *Maharsha* on the parallel at b. Hagigah 14b.
17. See Judah Goldin's wonderful essay: Goldin (1965: 7–8). Goldin claims that this is merely a congratulatory *topos* and adduces classical sources to which Prof. Lieberman added a few more. We will return to Goldin's essay in the next chapter, but on this point I am reluctant to agree.
18. Bar-Asher Siegel (2014: 138 n. 5–6).
19. Kahana (2006: 24, 86).
20. Four entered the Pardes: Ben Azzai, Ben Zoma, Aher, and Rabbi Akiva. One gazed and died. One gazed and was afflicted. One gazed and cut down the saplings. One went up in peace and went down in peace. Ben Azzai gazed and died. Scripture says about him: "Precious in the eyes of the Lord is the death of His faithful ones" (Ps 116:15). Ben Zoma gazed and was afflicted. Scripture says about him: "If you find honey, eat only what you need, lest, gorging yourself, you throw it up" (Prov 25:16). Elisha gazed and cut down the saplings. Scripture says about him: "Don't let your mouth bring your flesh into sin" (Eccles 5:5) (after Sefaria translation).
21. See also Stroumsa (2005: 121): "Indeed Jewish esoteric teachings are mostly expressed in the spiritual hermeneutics of the Old Testament."
22. In a different story in the same sugya, that same fire encircles two other students of Rabban Yoḥanan, R. Joshua and R. Eliezer, when they study the Torah, Prophets and Scripture—apparently in a nonmystical fashion, but see Goshen-Gottstein (2000; Kohelet Rabbah 7:8, Kipperwasser ed., pp. 48–49).
23. Zussman (2005).
24. To be distinguished from the tanna, a sage of the Mishnaic period.
25. See de Lange (1976); Niehoff (2016, 2020, 2021, 2022).
26. Kahana (2006: 60–64; 78–79).
27. *Deuterosis* is probably the translation of "mishna," an oral teaching, reflecting the root of *shana* in Hebrew—"recite again, a second time," and *deutero* in Greek.
28. Lawson (1957: 23). See Latin text, German translation, notes, and bibliography in Origen, Fürst, and Strutwolf (2016: 60–61).
29. I do wonder whether there has not been a metathesis of kerubim for merkabah.

30. "A story of Rabbi Yehoshua who was walking in the thoroughfare and Ben Zoma was coming toward him. He reached him but did not greet him. He said to him from where and to where Ben Zoma? He said to him: I was speculating on the Work of Creation, and there is not between the upper waters and the lower waters even a handsbreadth. As it is written "and the spirit of God hovered over the face of the waters (Genesis 1:2)." And Scripture says "Like an eagle who rouses his nestlings, hovering over his young (Deut. 32:11)." Just as an eagle hovers over the nest, touching and not touching, so too there is not even a handsbreadth between the upper waters and lower waters. Rabbi Yehoshua said to his students: "Ben Zoma is already outside." In a few days, Ben Zoma passed away" (after Sefaria translation).
31. Porphyry, *Life of Plotinus* 23 (Armstrong 1989 vol. 1: 71.)
32. Ibid., 10, p. 35.
33. Gruenwald (1987).
34. See Tropper (2013: 175–176), who calls it "an apparition." He cites also Kalmin (1999: 41).
35. Porphyry, *Life of Plotinus*, 14. Armstrong, in the footnote on p. 11, doubts that the Origen mentioned there is the church father (RZ).
36. Macleod (1971: 370).

Chapter 7

1. Weiss (2018) wants to distance the later dilation on the letters and creation in *Sefer Yezira* (seventh century in his view) from earlier rabbinic sources.
2. This is an ancient Near Eastern epithet; see Marmorstein (1937/1968: 185ff). Urbach (1975: 783 n. 43) brings an opinion that the translation Marmorstein relied upon was a mistranslation of the ancient Sumerian psalm, but he brings a different attestation from the *Enuma Elish* 4:21–22.
3. I note that in all the other creations of the six days there are verbs of doing and creating accompanying God's oral declaration. Only in these two, light and the assembling of the waters, is the creation portrayed as "God said ... and it was."
4. Rubin (1998).
5. Fraade (2023: 26–27), citing b. Sanhedrin 38b.
6. On the primordial language in Judaism and Christianity, see Rubin (1998); Badalanova Geller (2021); Moss (2010); and Eshel and Stone (1993).
7. Pesikta d'Rav Kahana, *bahodesh hashlishi* (Mandelbaum 1962: 223; Braude 1975: 248). Pesikta Rabbati 21, in the same vein, has a parable of a prince who spends time abroad and learns their language. Upon his return, the king speaks to him in the foreign language. Compare Esther Rabbah 4:12 (Tabori-Atzmon ed., 95) which calls it "the language of its (Israel's?) life," the vernacular.
8. *Saraph* literally derives from the word for fire. The Septuagint translates it *opsin* = a serpent, probably because a preceding verse, Numbers 21:6, states that God struck them with "*hanehashim haseraphim*," which the Septuagint translates as "deadly serpents."
9. The midrash claims that neither in Greek (*gune* for female, *anthrope* for male) nor Aramaic (*ita, gavra*) is there the same closeness of names between male and female as in Hebrew (*ish, isha*).
10. That is, a play on words. See Kogut (1982: 293–298).
11. Exposition of names and word play with names are prominent features in the Bible itself. The Bible abounds in "*midrash sheimot*," similar to Plautus's *nomen est omen*.

12. Compare Origen's Letter to Africanus where the argument is made that the text of Susanna in the LXX version of the book of Daniel could not have originally been written in Hebrew, since a word play there exists only in Greek (De Lange 1983: 516).
13. *Yakar* does not appear in the best manuscripts.
14. On the belief in the power of language, letter and scripts in diverse cultures, see T. Weiss, *Sefer Yesirah and Its Contexts* (Philadelphia: University of Pennsylvania Press, 2018), chapters 1 and 2.
15. Possibly better to translate as "interpreted." On the development of the verb to "open" (pataḥ) from the usual physical meaning to a more abstract one of interpretation from the Bible through the rabbis, see Mandel (2018).
16. Lieberman (1950/1962: 87).
17. If indeed this alternate explanation is in fact R. Hoshaya's as the scholarly consensus holds. The value added to R. Akiva's statement is the connection with Proverbs 8:30, the great oration by Wisdom that Ben Sira will go on to identify with Torah.
18. M. Hirshman, *Torah for the Entire World* (Hebrew) (Tel Aviv: Hakkibutz Hameuchad): 131.
19. See the ample bibliography in Sarit Kattan Gribetz and David M. Grossberg, *Genesis Rabbah in Text and Context* (Princeton, NJ: Princeton University Press, 2016): 1 n.1.
20. *Yefe Toar* commentary ad locum.
21. See Niehoff (2005), who, in a long line of scholars, sees this as R. Hoshaya's response to the parable in Philo, which Niehoff suggests is adapted in Origen. It is contended that R. Hoshaya, Origen's contemporary and fellow Caesarean, is rebutting the Origen's Christian reading. Because of the strange overlap with Paul above and also on the grounds that "the way of the world" is a formula much different from Philo's usage, I am less convinced that there is a borrowing or polemic here. Be that as it may, so many fine scholars have posited such that we should not rule out the possibility that the comparison was influenced by the *topos* in Philo and Origen.
22. Bacher (1891: 359).
23. See the usages listed in Albeck's meticulous introduction to Genesis Rabbah, p. 37. There are thirteen examples listed there. The ones opposing God's ways to that of a king of flesh and blood are pp. 5, 10–11, 25, 50, and 52 in the Theodor Albeck edition.
24. At Genesis Rabbah 1:5, scholars have attributed the phrase to Rav, though a close examination shows that the comparison is not at all a continuation of Rav's brief comment. The two exceptions in Genesis Rabbah where the comparison is almost surely of a named sage are at 1:12 (R. Yudan in the name of Aquilas) and 14:6 (R. Abba bar Kahana). The latter is not a comparison to a king of flesh and blood, but the former is indeed the exception.
25. Compare Fraenkel (1991: 73–77).
26. The biblical country *Shinar* is identified by this midrash as Babylonia. *Shinar* is read as a *notarikon*, a kind of shorthand, to mean "its youth," Babylonia Jewry's youth, who "look into the Torah" from their youth. This is a nod by our Land of Israel midrash to the great educational achievements of the Jews of Babylonia. Compare Elitzur (2014, 314 ff and especially pp. 317–318). This second usage seems to contradict the sense that the Torah is an artifact.
27. Thus Parma 2552, Cambridge Or. 786. The other manuscripts read: Shmuel ben R. Yosi. My thanks to Prof. Arnon Atzmon for sharing his synopsis of the manuscripts with me.
28. Yonatan Moss does an excellent job of charting the different historical opinions on whether juxtaposition is to be interpreted and the ensuant interpretive debate of

whether one can both hold the opinion that the Torah is not ordered chronologically and still interpret juxtaposition ("Disorder in the Bible: Rabbinic Responses and Responsibilities," *JSQ* 19 [2012]: 104–128). See further note 18 on Origen's position. See also Isaac B. Gottlieb, *Order in the Bible: The Arrangement of the Torah in Rabbinic and Medieval Jewish Commentary* (Hebrew) (Ramat Gan: Bar Ilan University Press; Jerusalem: Magnes Press, 2009), 6 n. 14, for an important contribution and bibliography.
29. W. Z. Bacher, "The Church Father Origen, and Rabbi Hoshaya," *Jewish Quarterly Review* 3 (1891): 357–360; "*Die Agada der Palästinensichen Amoräer*, 3 vols. (Strassburg: Karl J. Trübner, 1896), 2:31. Bacher also firmly affirmed the antiquity of this passage, and I follow his lead.
30. Abraham Joshua Heschel, *Theology of Ancient Judaism* (Hebrew), 3 vols. (London:Soncino, 1962–1990), 2: 361 n. 10–11. The editors of Heschel's *Heavenly Torah: As Refracted through the Generations*, ed. and trans. Gordon Tucker with Leonard Levin (New York: Continuum, 2005), 590, deleted the passage and glossed it with n. 5.
31. Gershom Scholem, *On the Kabbalah and Its Symbolism*, trans. Ralph Manheim (New York: Schocken, 1965), 37, published in a previous and slightly different form in *Diogenes* 4, no. 15 (1956): "The conception of the God's name as the highest concentration of divine power forms a connecting link between two sets of ideas, the one originally associated with magic, the other pertaining to mystical speculation as such. The idea of the magic structure and nature of the Torah may be found long before the Kabbalah, in a relatively early midrash, for example, where in commenting on Job 28:13: "No man knoweth its order," Rabbi Eleazar declares: "The various sections of the Torah were not given in their correct order." Scholem, in n. 1, also references Bacher, *Die Agada der Palästinensichen Amoräer*, 31. I owe this reference to Yuval Demalach and thank Prof. Oded Yisraeli for helping me to relocate it and for Oded's thoughts about whether indeed one need connect our passage to Nachmanides's views of the names of God hidden in the letters of Torah, as Scholem did.
32. According to most of the manuscripts, after correcting Shmuel to Yishmael ben R. Yosi and therefore Rebbe is Judah the Patriarch.
33. Menahem I. Kahana, *Sifre on Numbers: An Annotated Edition* (Hebrew), 3 vols. (Jerusalem: Magnes Press, 2015), 2: 1086.
34. Ecclesiastes Rabbah 3:11—God hid (*he'elim*) the Name from them. See Ephraim E. Urbach, *The Sages: Their Concepts and Beliefs*, trans. Israel Abrahams, 2 vols. (Jerusalem: Magnes Press, 1987), chapter 7.

Chapter 8

1. See recently Bar-On (2017: 62–64), with a limited bibliography. Hirshman (2009: 17–30).
2. This was the title of the emerging Torah scholar—a pupil of the wise. The manuscript tradition has the sages in the plural, but it was shortened in later printings to the more familiar *talmid ḥaham*, which then was translated as "a wise pupil"! On admission requirements, see Safrai (1976: 949–950 n. 1).
3. *Zer* meaning a wreath is popular in the early medieval piyyut, religious poetry. It would seem that the pun by R. Yoḥanan reading *zer* molding as a wreath is unattested elsewhere in early rabbinic literature.
4. On merit *zkh*, see Kister (2007: 393–394).

5. The warning is, of course, to the students of the sages themselves, but often in order not to say something deprecatory about those students, it is phrased in a circumlocution that the Talmud calls "hanging one's curse on someone else."
6. I have translated relying on the parallel in b. Shabbat 88b, which opposes doing it with one's right or left (hand?).
7. In one of the two Yemenite manuscripts (Enelow 270), this saying is attributed to the Babylonian sage Rava whose following comment has an identical formulation. All the other manuscripts including the Yemenite Enelow 271 attribute this to R. Yoḥanan.
8. See also Marmorstein (1920/1968: 78 n. 179).
9. See H. Yalon. "*Pilpel* . . . In Hebrew and Aramaic," (Hebrew) *Tarbiz* 6 (1935): 223–229, http://www.jstor.org/stable/23583706.
10. Sin fearing and God fearing are two very different things (see Hirshman 1994). Yet here they are conflated. See also de Villier Pieter 2020.
11. Moore (1927: 2.96).
12. Büchler (1909?: 63).
13. The prayer was adopted in the Ashkenazi ritual of announcing the new month on the Sabbath.
14. b. Pesahim 50b. See especially Krumbein's (2010) analysis of the term.
15. Büchler (1967: 69). This later Hebrew translation of Büchler's (1909) work goes beyond the English of the 1909 publication. I have yet to find the source for these revisions.
16. Büchler (1967: 70).
17. Sifre Deuteronomy 306, Finkestein ed.: 337.
18. Attribution to R. Yishmael is only here and not in parallel Sifre Numbers 15 and is far from certain. See Kahana (2011: 2, 160–161).
19. Lieberman (1961: 206), citing Bacher, REJ 38 (1899: 39 ff).
20. Roth-Gerson (1987: 110) (Hebrew; translation mine).
21. My translation of the title. I am reacting to the notion in the title of the lecture of a dark side (*afel*) of the Torah. The lecture was given at Hebrew University, Mt Scopus, on February 20, 2024. Professor Kister's masterful comparison of the motif in Second-Temple Pauline and Rabbinic literature will, I trust, be published in the near future.

Chapter 9

1. Simmons (2015: 107). See Birnbaum's (2016) wonderful review of the topic.
2. Hirshman (1999, 2000). Segal (1995). Compare Berthelot (2018). Also Sandberg (2017).
3. Weinfeld (1964); Levenson (1996).
4. See M. Kahana, *Sifre on Numbers: An Annotated Commentary*, vol. 4 (Jerusalem: Magnes): 731 n. 251; Cover (2016: 630–632).
5. See the liturgy for the Sabbath morning Amidah up until our own time.
6. Shafat (2014: 22).
7. Cf. Philo, *Congr.* 63–70; Jesus's sower's parable Matthew 13:18–23, Mark 4:13–20, Luke 8:11–15.
8. Safrai (1970: 64); Friedman (2010: 422).
9. See Hayes (2022: 136 n. 134) quoting Menahem Kahana; Zlotnick (1988).
10. Falls (1965: 210). See also chapter 28.
11. *Theophany* 2.76 cited in Simmons (2015: 95).

12. See Wright (1923) *The Letters of Julian*, Letter 22 430d: cited by Wilfand (2017: 202). The letter was quoted at the beginning of Chapter 3, on charity.
13. Mirsky (2011).

Chapter 10

1. Hebrew *ve'anvehu* is rendered by NJPS as "enshrine," from the root *nvh*, which appears again in Exodus 15:13 "your holy (*nvh*) abode." Other translations see it in parallel "to exalt" and translate "praise" from the word "to beautify," *na'eh*.
2. See further Rosen-Zvi (2008).
3. Mechilta of R. Yishmael, *Beshalaḥ, Shira* 3 Horovitz-Rabin ed., (126–127). One cannot properly read this section of the Mechilta without studying Judah Goldin (1990), a brilliant and patient reading of the Mechilta's commentary on the Song at the Sea. It remains the single best guide to understanding how midrashic exegesis works. It was first published by Yale University Press in 1971 and and is as instructive today as it was then.
4. Chapter 6 above and Hirshman (2000).
5. The Genizah fragment BL OR 5559A divides the *parasha* into smaller sections and numbers them consecutively. This division was lost in the manuscripts and printed editions.
6. Boyarin (1990: 120–121).
7. Bar-Or (2011: 59–61).
8. "Creator" translates the Hebrew *konav*. Though familiar, it and its alternate form *kono* are very rare in tannaitic collections, appearing less than ten times (four times in Mishna and Tosefta) and in midrashic collections, only in those associated with the school of R. Yishmael (Sifre Numbers 99; 139; Mechilta of R. Yishmael, Horowitz ed., 88, see variants). The idea of beautifying oneself in the eyes of God appears again in Mechilta Deuteronomy 12:28 and might also be connected with R. Yishmael. See further Kahana (2018), especially pp. 573–574.
9. Lewy (1876: 23). In his essay on "*Mishnat Abba Shaul*," Lewy praises Abba Shaul's high moral stature and spirituality as reflected in this and his few other aggadic statements. Lewy cites Sifra Kedoshim, where Abba Shaul glosses the verse "You shall be holy for I the Lord am holy" (Lev 19:2) with the comment: "the *pamalia* (*familia* = entourage) of the king—what should it do? Imitate the king."
10. This addition is not to be found in any of the manuscripts, as opposed to R. Akiva's similar formulation later on where it reads "I will speak."
11. These final words are in all the manuscripts but missing in Genizah fragment BL OR 5559b. Since R. Akiva's statement a few lines down begins the exact same way, the omission would distinguish the two statements from one another. The parallel in Mechilta of R. Simon reads like the Genizah fragment with R. Yosi immediately preceding R. Akiva. This shift in order might indicate a later addition in both texts, but as it stands, R. Yose would speak of singing God's praises while R. Akiva would stress singing God's praises before the nations of the world.
12. This is the version in ms Munich, Genizah, and the first printed edition. The Oxford ms passed over the word. In ms Castanesa, it is corrected to *naveh*. The earlier tradition is puzzling and needs further reflection.
13. The manuscripts (Munich, Oxford, Castanesa, and first printed edition) all read some form of *benevuotav* = in his prophecies. Only the Genizah reads *nevotav* like R. Yose above.

14. Genizah reads: "all of this praise."
15. "In those days ten people from all languages and nations will take firm hold of one Jew by the hem of his robe and say, 'Let us go with you, because we have heard that God is with you.'"
16. Substituting *lamed* for *nun*, a common exchange of sonant letters.
17. Parallel in Mechilta of R. Shimon has tabernacle and the editors of Mechilta of R. Yishmael rightly suggest that the Temple should be added there, similar to m. Ta'anit 4:8.
18. The *parasha* continues with a new series of interpretations of the verse from the word "*eli*," taken as the attribute of mercy, a parable of Israel being a queen, the daughter of kings ("the God of our ancestors") and R. Elazar ben Simon speaking of God's name being sanctified when Israel does God's bidding (*ve'aromemenhu*—extol him). Finally, the *parasha* closes with an anonymous homily where Israel addresses God directly and asserts the she praises God not only for the past but for miracles in every generation.
19. But see Yaakov Efrati in M. Z. Kadari, *Erchei Leshon Sifrut Hazal* (Ramat Gan: Bar Ilan University Press, 1974): 21–22, who suggests that the meaning of the root might be "I will be like him."
20. See Marmorstein (1950: 110 ff). Compare Henry Chadwick's characterization of the *Sentences of Sextus* (Chadwick 1959: 97): "The believing soul is to pursue the moral ideal, which is to be made like unto God (44ff.). Yet that impossible divine life is far distant from this mortal existence swayed by passion and earthiness. Accordingly, the first task of exhortation is to awaken the soul to self-realization, to arouse it to know to how high and weighty an office it is called..."
21. Unless the Genizah fragment retains the original form of R. Yose's statement. See note 11 above.
22. I have raised the possibility that the continuation might not be authored by Akiva, but scholarship seems unanimous in attributing it to R. Akiva.
23. See Boyarin (1990:121 ff), who unpacked the elegance of this complex midrash. He did not stress the role of the nations and the antipathy toward them that turns R. Akiva's interpretation of glorifying God before the nations into shutting the door in their face, presumably unless they convert.
24. Ibid., 122.
25. Mintz (1981: 189).

Index

For the benefit of digital users, indexed terms that span two pages (e.g., 52–53) may, on occasion, appear on only one of those pages.

act of the chariot (*maaseh merkavah*), 58, 62–64, 65
act of creation (*maaseh bereishit*), 58, 62–63, 65–66
affection (*ḥiba*), 39, 43, 45
agapé (love), 37. *See also* eros
aggadic midrash 2–3, 6–7, 71, 116. *See also* midrash aggada
R. Akiva, 2–3, 5–7, 11–12, 13, 14–15, 16, 17–18, 25–26, 35, 43, 45, 60–61, 62–63, 67, 72, 73, 74–76, 78–80, 86, 96, 101, 102, 104, 110, 111–12, 116
Amora, Amoraim, 3–4, 7–8, 25, 27–28, 29, 31, 38, 44, 45, 78–79, 85, 89, 96
amoraic period, 1–2, 6–8, 53–54, 99–100, 101, 102
Aristotle, 47–48

Babylonia, 3–4, 16, 45, 47–48, 115
Bar Kochva, 5
baraita/baraitot, 3–4, 66
R. Benaya, 88–89, 90–93
Ben Sira, 21–22, 73

Caesarea, 3–4, 5–7, 36–37, 53–54, 74–75, 103–4
chariot mysticism, 61, 62. *See also*, act of the chariot
charity (*zedaka*), 6, 22, 25–28, 29, 30, 31–32, 83

charity basket *(kupa)*, 25
charity plate (*tamḥui*), 25
Christian literature, vii–viii, 5, 35
Christian movement, 4, 7–8, 91–92, 115
Christian and pagan universalist debate, 104
creation, 7, 14, 49–50, 58, 60, 62–64, 65, 70–71, 73, 74–76, 79–80, 96. *See also* act of creation (*maaseh bereishit*)

daimon (heavenly spirit), 66
dalma (drama, story), 24–25, 28, 30
derech tova (the good path), *derech yeshara* (the right path), 50–51
Deuteronomy and education, 35
Dinah, 39–41
doreish sheimot (interpret names), 71–72

Early Christianity, 35, 36–37
R. Elazar, 51, 59–60, 78
R. Elazar b. Arach, 49–50, 59–60, 61–62, 63–64, 65
R. Eliezer / R. Eliezer ben Hyrcanus, 5–6, 91–92, 95, 106–7, 109
Epictetus, 51–52
Epicurus, 47–48
eros, 37, 41, 42, 110
erotic love, 35, 39, 41, 42, 45
"evil inclination" (*yetzer hara*), 42

136 INDEX

Fear of Heaven, 45, 85, 86–87, 88, 89, 93

Galilee, Sea of, 47–48
God's Torah, 44–45, 75
Gog and Magog, 77
Greco-Roman culture, 29, 54
Greco-Roman literature, vii–viii, 1, 5, 47–48
Greco-Roman philosophy, 6–7, 47–48, 50–51, 54–55

Halacha lemoshe misinai, 14–15. *See also* law of Moses from Sinai
R. Ḥama, 30
ḥaye nefashot (regarding the lives of people), 27–28. *See also nefashot*
Holy of Holies, 35, 45, 66, 67. *See also* Song of Songs
R. Hoshaya Rabba, 29

Jerome, St. 5–6
Jesus, 16, 36–37, 91–92
Jewish Christians, 5–6
Jewish liturgy, 12–13
Josephus, 16, 18, 19, 30, 54
R. Joshua, 59–60, 61, 62, 65–66
R. Joshua ben Levi, 10–11, 12, 13, 15, 16–17, 78–80, 89, 92–93
Jubilees, 9, 13, 14, 19, 70–71
Judah the Patriarch, Rabbi, Rebbe 2, 3–4, 16, 50–51, 78–79, 91–92
Julian, Emperor, 21
juxtaposition, 78–79

Kupa. See charity basket

Land of Israel, 3–4, 6–8, 25, 26–27, 38–39, 44, 45, 85, 86, 89, 90, 92–93, 96, 97, 115, 116

Land of Israel Amoraim, 25, 38, 44, 45, 85, 89, 90, 116. *See also* amora, amoraim
late antiquity, vii–viii, 1–2, 4, 5–6, 15, 16, 47, 54, 79–80, 106, 114, 115, 117–18
law of Moses from Sinai *(Halacha lemoshe misinai),* 10, 14–15, 16
Life (and death), 26–28, 30–32, 35–36, 40, 45, 79–80, 84–85, 86, 89, 90, 92, 93, 118–19, 124n.23, 127n.14. *See also ḥaye* and *nefashot*
Lydda, Lod 3–4, 30

maaseh bereishit. See act of creation
maaseh merkavah. See act of the chariot
Maimonides, 54–55
Midrash Aggada (Midrash of non-legal nature), 3–4
Midrash Halacha (Midrash of the Law), 2–3
Midrash Tannaim, 2–4
minim (heretics), 91
Monabases, King, 30, 31–32
Moses, 3–5, 6, 9, 10, 11–13, 14–15, 16–18, 35, 39–40, 43, 71–72, 116
Mount Sinai/Sinai, 6, 8, 9, 10, 11–12, 13, 14–15, 16–19, 96, 97, 101
Mysticism, 7, 47, 58, 59–60, 62–64, 66, 78–79

nefashot (lives, souls), 26, 27–28, 30, 31–32
New Testament
 Matthew 6:19–21, 30
 Matthew 22:37, 36
 Mark 4:19–23, 131n.7
 Mark 7, 16
 Mark 12:28–30, 36
 Luke 8:11–15, 131n.7

1Corinthians 13:1–8, 36
Galatians 3:24, 74–75

Oenomaus 47–48
Oral law, 2–3, 11–12, 15–16, 17–18, 47–48, 54–55, 58, 62–63, 64, 115, 116
Origen, 5–7, 36–37, 41, 53–54, 64–65, 66, 67, 73, 74–75, 103–4

pardes (orchard), 62, 63–64
parnas, parnasim (communal officers), 23, 24, 26, 27–28, 32
Particularism, 96–97, 102, 104, 111–12
Pedagogy, 54
Pharaoh, 39–40, 41
Philo of Alexandria, 53–54, 73, 74–75
Plato, 50–51
Plotinus, 66
Porphyry, 66, 95, 103–4

rabbinic culture, 54–55
rabbinic Judaism, 15–16, 35, 89, 95
rabbinic learning, 2–4, 6–7, 64–65, 77, 79–80
rabbinic literature, 1, 3–5, 6–7, 8, 10–11, 27–28, 35, 37, 38, 39–40, 43, 47–48, 52–55, 58, 64, 79–80, 91–92, 106, 112, 115, 116–19
rabbinic religion, 1–2, 5, 6, 8, 112
rhetoric (and aggada), 2–3, 6, 53–54, 117
right way (*derech yeshara*), 50–51
Roman Empire, 4, 21, 31–32, 49–50, 54, 66, 95, 102, 103–4

Sassanian Empire, 104, 115
Second Temple, 6, 9, 13, 14, 16, 21–22, 35, 44–45, 62–63, 73, 96
Second Temple, destruction of the, 9, 15–16

Septuagint, 43
R. Simon ben Lakish/Reish Lakish, 6–7, 38–41, 42, 43, 45, 87
Song of Songs, 6–7, 35, 36–37, 40–41, 45, 64–65, 67, 109, 111–12
   in New Testament 36–37
stam (anonymous statements in rabbinic literature), 3–4
Sura academy, 45, 89

talmid ḥachamim (student of the sages), 83, 84, 130n.2
Talmudic literature, 15, 102
tamḥui (the common platter). *See* charity plate
Tannaim, 2, 5, 78–79
tannaitic literature, 3–4, 7–8, 25–26, 61, 90, 102, 115
tannaitic midrash, 8, 15–16, 64–65, 98, 106
tannaitic period, 1–3, 7–8, 17–18, 25–26, 53–54, 62–64, 99–100
Tiberias, 31–32
Tobit, 21–22
Torah, 2–3, 7, 9, 11–12, 13–14, 16, 17–18, 39–40, 44–45, 50–51, 70, 72, 73, 74–80, 85, 86–87, 89–90, 92, 96–97, 99–100, 101, 129–30n.28
Torah lishma (Torah study for its own sake), 90–91
Torah study, 7–8, 49–50, 83, 85, 88–89, 90, 91, 92, 93, 96, 112

Universalism, 7–8, 95, 96–97, 99–100, 101, 102, 103–4, 106–7, 111–12

Wisdom, 5–6, 37, 44, 51, 54–55, 73, 75, 76–77, 80, 89, 93, 118–19, 125n.20, 129n.17
Writings, 21–22

Written Torah, 12, 18, 47–48, 54–55, 115

yetzer hara. See evil inclination

R. Yishmael, 2–3, 7–8, 15, 62–63, 78–79, 91, 96, 101, 106, 109

R. Yoḥanan, vii–viii, 38, 83, 85

Rabban Yoḥanan ben Zakkai, 5–7, 27–28, 31–32, 38–39, 47, 48, 49–51, 52, 58, 59–61, 62, 63–64

R. Yose from Damascus, 110

R. Yosi, 27–28, 78–79, 90–91

Zedaka. See charity

Rabbinic Sources

Mishna:
   Avoda Zara 2:5, 127n.14
   Avot 1:1, 17–18
      1:3, 88
      3:14, 43–44, 96
   Ḥagiga 1:8–2:2, 62–63
      2:1, 58
   Horayot 3:7, 32
   Kerithot 3:7, 127n.14
   Pe'ah 8:7–9, 22, 24
   Rosh Hashana 1:2, 95
   Sheqalim 5:1, 23
   Taanit 4:8, 133n.17
   Tamid 4:1, 35

Tosefta:
   Eduyot 1:14, 86
   Ḥagigah 2:1–7, 58
      2:2, 47
   Ḥalla 1:6, 127n.15
   Horayot 2:6, 124n.23
   Ḥullin 2:2, 91–92
      2:20–21, 2:24, 5–6
   Me'ilah 1:15, 127n.15
   Niddah 6:6, 60–61
   Pe'ah 3:2, 127n.15
      4:18, 30
   Pesaḥim 2:16, 60–61, 126n.8
   Shabbat 13:5, 91
   Sotah 9, 67
      13:9, 66
   Ta'anit 1:11, 61
   Yevamot 8:7

Midrash Halakhah:

   Mekhilta of Rabbi Yishmael
      Bo 16, 61
      Jethro, tractate Amalek 2, 127n.15
      Jethro, tractate Baḥodesh, 9, 101
      Ki-Tisa 1, 127n.21

   Mekhilta Deuteronomy 12:28, 132n.8

   Sifra Kedoshim 4:12, 124n.1, 132n.9
   Sifre Numbers 15, 131n.18
      75, 61
      99, 132n.8
      131, 78–79
   Sifre Deuteronomy 41, 90–91
      49, 41
      306, 88–89, 90, 131n.17
      311, 98
      343, 98
      345, 96

Babylonian Talmud:
   Bava Metziah 81a, 71, 84a, 124n.7
   Bava Batra 91b, 31–32
   Berakhot 7a, 66
      16b, 45, 89
   Eruvin 54a, 89
      54b, 125n.19
   Ḥagigah 14b, 127n.16
   Ketubot 67a, 124n.23
   Menaḥot 29b, 9, 10–11
      99b, 44–45

140 RABBINIC SOURCES

Babylonian Talmud (cont.)
Megilah 7a, 79–80
Pesaḥim 50b, 131n.14
Sanhedrin 38b 128n.5
  59a, 96
  65a, 79–80
Shabbat 31a, 87
  88b, 131n.6
  88b–89a, 10–11, 12, 122n.2
Sotah 21a, 89
Ta'anit 19b, 31–32
Yoma 124n.7
  72a, 93
  72b, 83

Jerusalem Talmud:
Berachot 5:1, 9a 44
  8:6, 12c, 39
Kiddushin 1:7, 4–5
Pe'ah 1:1, 123–24n.21
  8:8, 24
  8:9, 24
  8, 22, 31, 32
Rosh Hashana 3:9, 59a 71–72
Sheqalim 24
Terumot 8:9, 46c 38–39

Midrash Rabbah:
Ecclesiastes Rabbah 3:11, 130n.34
  7:8, 127n.22
  10:16, 38–39

Esther Rabbah 4:12, 128n.7
Genesis Rabbah 40, 71–72, 78, 86
  1:1, 72–73
  1:5, 129n.24
  1:7, 75
  9:7, 42
  37:4, 42, 75
  31:14, 71
  80:8, 39
  90:2, 39–40
Leviticus Rabbah 1, 43
  13, 96–97
  22:4, 79–80
  29:1, 95
  34, 26–27, 31–32
  34:2 32, 123n.5
Ruth Rabbah 2:14, 122n.4
Song of Songs Rabbah, 35, 122n.3
  6, 4, 2, 76–77
  8, 10, 122n.2
  8:9, 124n.7

Midrash Tanchuma Tisa 16, 9, 16–18, 122n.14

Midrash Tehillim, 79–80
Pesikta d'Rav Kahana baḥodesh 70–71, 128n.7
  vayehi 1:6, 76–77

Pesiqta Rabbati 21, 128n.7